1

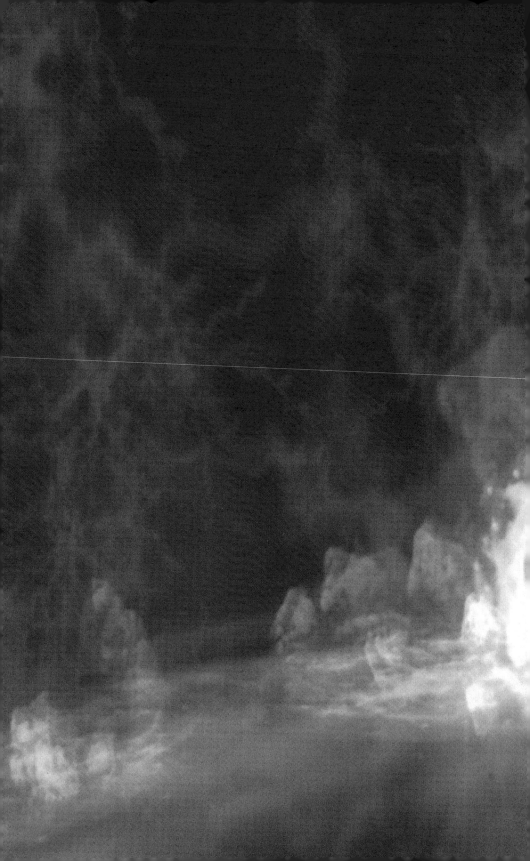

*Only through a gifted
lightworker, the spiritual
world can be reached,
and the thin line separating
goodness and evil can
be defined.*

*Although science
is the pragmactic
tool to understand
our universe,
it would never penetrate
the realm of ultimate
wisdom and cosmic
awareness; this is the task
of lightworkers.*

Date Publication: December 13, 2014.
Published by Times Square Press, New York.
Printed in the United States of America.

Maximillien de Lafayette's books are available in the following formats:
1-Amazon Kindle edition at www.amazon.com
2-Paperback available at lulu.com, amazon.com, banes&noble, and worldwide.

Author's website:
www.maximilliendelafayettebibliography.org/biblio
Email: delafayette6@aol.com

2015 BEST PSYCHICS, MEDIUMS AND LIGHTWORKERS IN THE UNITED STATES.

Based upon
The 4th national & international election/vote of the United States and the world's best mediums, psychics, healers, astrologers and lightworkers 2014-2015

The national and international vote began on September 25, 2014 and ended on November 25, 2014 at 1:00 AM New York Time.

Staff
Marla Cohen
Judith Goldsmith
Samantha Rozen
Shoshanna Rozenstein
David Blum
Fabiola Rossi
Liza Coleman
Peggy North

Data
Melinda Pomerleau

Book layout & Design by
Fabiola Rossi
Rome, Italy

TIMES SQUARE PRESS
New York

Warning

Before you call any psychic, medium, astrologer, lightworker, find out first if his/her name isin this book! It's your money. Be cautious. Be smart. Play it safe!! Avoid scammers! Bear in mind that there are thousands upon thousands of lightworkers in the United States, and almost 1,456.000 practitioners in the world.
Do you really know who are the best, the honest, the caring, the most effective, the most expensive, the most affordable, and who are the fraudulent and deceptive ones?
Perhaps you do to a certain degree. But at Times Square Press we know best, thanks to our unlimited resources, our data base, years and years of investigation and research, our contact and communications with lightworkers from around the world.

Those who were nominated in various categories are the choice of the public. Read this book very attentively, and keep it handy, if you are still searching for the most reliable lightworkers.

*** *** ***

DON'T CALL A PSYCHIC BEFORE
YOU READ THIS BOOK.

OFFICIAL STATEMENT: PLEASE READ RIGHT NOW
AND CAREFULLY!

The results are not based upon packaged fame, TV, radio and media's propaganda, and maximum exposure organized and promoted by public relations firms and agents, but rather on consumers, clients, and the general public recommendations, satisfaction, and ultimately, their votes.

The elections/votes are the public's choice and word-of-mouth. Nevertheless, Times Square Press does NOT in any shape or form, categorically endorse the choice of those who participated in the vote. It was the public choice and NOT or our publishing house's choice, selection and/or decision.
The votes/election echoe the voice of people from around the globe, and not Times Square Press, its affiliates or the author.

The votes and nominations began on September 25, 2014 and ended on November 25, 2014 at 1:00 AM, New York time.

2015 BEST PSYCHICS, MEDIUMS AND LIGHTWORKERS IN THE UNITED STATES

Based upon
The 4th national & international election/vote of the
United States and the world's best mediums, psychics,
healers, astrologers and lightworkers 2014-2015

Maximillien de Lafayette

ORGANIZED BY TIMES SQUARE PRESS

Jointly Published by
Times Square Press
Stars Illustrated Magazine

New York
2014

Table of Contents

LA CRÈME DE LA CRÈME
The 5 stars and 4 stars lightworkers

According to the latest statistics of the American Federation of certified Psychics and Mediums Inc. www.amcpm.org (A non-profit, official organization and state approved) there are over 1,250.000 (Latest Figure) practitioners in the world, but few deserve our ultimate respect, trust, and admiration.

La crème de la crème list includes the jewels of the crown, the best of the very best in the business; lightworkers who are in the top 5 and top 10 in each category, and/or who have received 5 stars and 4 stars rating. Listing is established in conformity with the choice, opinion, acknowledgment, and vote of customers, clients and peers from around the world.

And not according to acknowledgement and certification (Approved, tested, blah blah blah) displayed on the Internet in paid listings and directories of psychics and mediums, which usually are given to psychics and mediums by the business owner (s) of said commercial directories, who are just business persons, trying to make a living by selling advertisement space in their Internet directories to lightworkers of all kinds and sorts. It is not against the law, it is perfectly legal, but in many instances, highly suspicious business transactions, because the business owner of Internet directories of psychics and mediums is the same person who tests and approves psychics and mediums, later to list them if they continue to pay a monthly fee.

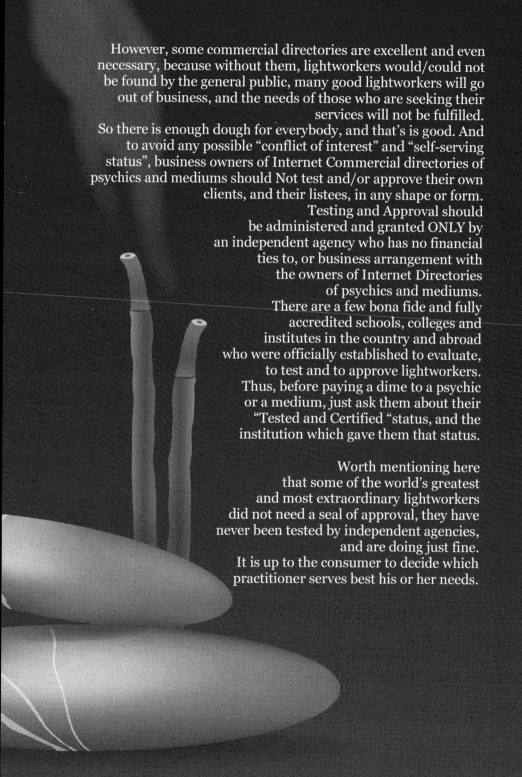

However, some commercial directories are excellent and even necessary, because without them, lightworkers would/could not be found by the general public, many good lightworkers will go out of business, and the needs of those who are seeking their services will not be fulfilled.

So there is enough dough for everybody, and that's is good. And to avoid any possible "conflict of interest" and "self-serving status", business owners of Internet Commercial directories of psychics and mediums should Not test and/or approve their own clients, and their listees, in any shape or form.

Testing and Approval should be administered and granted ONLY by an independent agency who has no financial ties to, or business arrangement with the owners of Internet Directories of psychics and mediums.

There are a few bona fide and fully accredited schools, colleges and institutes in the country and abroad who were officially established to evaluate, to test and to approve lightworkers.

Thus, before paying a dime to a psychic or a medium, just ask them about their "Tested and Certified "status, and the institution which gave them that status.

Worth mentioning here that some of the world's greatest and most extraordinary lightworkers did not need a seal of approval, they have never been tested by independent agencies, and are doing just fine.

It is up to the consumer to decide which practitioner serves best his or her needs.

In this roster, no such thing takes place; no paid fees, no monthly dues, no commercial listing, and no advertisement for and by psychics and mediums.

Results came directly from the mouth and heart of consumers, and peers. The list of La Crème de la Crème is also based upon the score and "stars-rating" each lightworker has received at the 4th National and International Vote for the Best Lightworkers in the United States. This is the list of the most respected, trusted, decent and effective practitioners in the world.

And how about those who received 3 stars? Should we consider them as a "Second Choice"? Absolutely not. Many of them are fantastic, effective and friendly, but were not lucky this year.

*** *** ***

Americans who made the list by alphabetical order:

A

- Abby Rose (USA) Category: Spirit Artist. 4 stars
- Abby Rose Newman (USA) Category: Psychic. 4 stars
- Adrienne Miles (USA) Category: Psychic. 4 stars
- Alexandra Juliani (USA) Category: Healer. 5 stars
- Alexandra Shaw (USA) Category: Feng Shui practitioner. 4 stars
- Allison Dubois (USA) Category: Psychic. 5 stars
- Allison Hayes (USA) Category: Psychic. 5 stars
- Amelia Armstrong (USA) Category: Psychic. 4 stars
- Amelia Pisano Scozzari (Canada/USA) Category: Psychic. 4 stars
- Amy Cavanaugh (USA) Category: Healer. 4 stars
- Amy Diggins (USA) Category: Medium. 5 stars
- Andrew Brewer (USA) Category: Psychic. 4 stars
- Andy Young (USA) Category: Tarot Reader. 4 stars
- Angela Bixbi (USA) Category: Angel Reader. 5 stars
- Angela Bixby (USA) Category: Psychic. 5 stars
- Angela Bixby, Reverend (USA) Category: Life-Coach Psychic. 5 stars
- Angela Kruszka. Category: Tarot Reader. 4 stars

15

- Angela Lucy (USA) Category: Tarot Reader. 4 stars
- Anita Rosenberg (USA): Category: Feng Shui practitioner. 5 stars
- Ann Cutler, MA (USA) Category: Dream Interpreter. 4 stars
- Annette Betcher (USA) Category: Pet Psychic/Animal Communicator. 4 stars
- Anny Rose Newman (USA) Category: Spirit Artist. 4 stars
- Anthony Morgann (USA) Category: Healer. 4 stars
- Antoinette Hemmerich (USA) Category: Reiki Practitioner. 5 stars
- Antoinette Hemmerich (USA) Category: Reiki Practitioner. 5 stars
- April Ashbrook (USA) Category: Psychic. 5 stars
- Arsène André (France) Category: Psychic. 4 stars
- Artie Hoffman (USA) Category: Angel Reader. 5 stars
- Ashlei Yatron (USA) Category: Psychic. 4 stars
- Ashley Riley (USA) Category: Healer. 4 stars
- Frank Andrews (USA) Category: Psychic. 5 stars

B

- B. Anne Gehman, Reverend (USA) Category: Medium. 5 stars
- Barbara Anderson (USA) Category: Angel Reader. 5 stars
- Barbara Brennan (USA) Category: Healer. 5 stars
- Barbara DeLong (USA) Category: Pet Psychic/Animal Communicator. 4 stars
- Barbara Mackey (USA) Category: Psychic. 4 stars
- Barbara Morrison (USA) Category: Pet Psychic/Animal Communicator. 4 stars
- Barbara Rawson (USA) Category: Pet Psychic/Animal Communicator. 5 stars
- Bee Herz (USA) Category: Psychic. 4 stars
- Bella Mason (USA) Category: Psychic. 5 stars
- Belle Salisbury (USA) Category: Medium. 5 stars
- Benjamin Spock, MD (USA) Category: Healer. 5 stars
- Betsy Cohen (USA) Category: Psychic. 4 stars

- Bill Northern (USA) Category: Pet Psychic/Animal Communicator. 4 stars
- Bj Haggerty (USA) Category: Ghost Hunter. 5 stars
- Bj Haggerty (USA) Category: Paranormal Researcher. 5 stars
- stars
- Bob Marks (USA) Category: Astrologer. 4 stars
- Brenton Harris (USA) Category: Dream Interpreter. 4 stars
- Briana Brooks (USA) Category: Angel Reader. 5 stars

C

- Carla Baron (USA) Category: Psychic. 4 stars
- Carmen Harra, PhD (USA) Category: Psychic. 5 stars
- Carol Bouteraon (France) Category: Pet Psychic/Animal Communicator. 5 stars
- Carol Gurney (USA) Category: Pet Psychic/Animal Communicator. 5 stars
- Carol Ritberger (USA) Category: Healer. 4 stars
- Caroline Musial (USA) Category: Reiki Practitioner. 5 star
- Carolyn B. Coleridge, MSW, LCSW (USA) Category: Healer. 5 stars
- Carolyn Myss. (USA) Category: Healer. 5 stars
- Carrie-Anne Hartley Silkowski (USA) Category: Medium. 4 stars
- Cassandra Larsen (USA) Category: Medium. 4 stars
- Cassandra Larsen (USA) Category: Psychic. 4 stars
- Catherine Fergusson (USA) Category: Pet Psychic/Animal Communicator. 4 stars
- Cathy Towle (USA) Category: Medium. 5 stars
- Celia Caulfield (USA) Category: Healer. 4 stars
- Chantal Cochard (France) Category: Medium. 4 stars
- Char Margolis (USA) Category: Psychic. 5 stars
- Charlene Hicks (USA) Category: Medium. 4 stars
- Charles Lightwalker (USA) Category: Healer. 4 stars
- Chef Sessy (USA) Category: Healer. 4 stars
- Cheryl Murphy (USA) Category: Angel Reader. 5 stars

- Chinhee Park (USA) Category: Psychic. 5 stars
- Chip Coffey (USA) Category: Psychic. 4 stars
- Chris Avery Cole (USA) Category: Psychic. 4 stars
- Christina Nelson (USA) Category: Pet Psychic/Animal Communicator. 4 stars
- Clarissa Bernhardt. (USA) Category: Astrologer. 4 stars
- Claudia Johnson (USA) Category: Healer. 5 stars
- Claudia Johnson (USA) Category: Psychic. 4 stars
- Clyde Lewis (USA) Category: Best Paranormal Radio Show Hosts in the US. 5 stars
- Clyde Lewis (USA) Category: Paranormal Researcher. 5 stars
- Colette Baron Reid (USA) Category: Healer. 4 stars
- Colette Baron-Reid (USA) Category: Psychic. 5 stars
- Concetta Bertoldi (USA) Category: Medium. 5 stars
- Coral Ryder (USA) Category: Spirit Artist. 4 stars
- Corbie Mitleid (USA) Category: Psychic. 5 stars
- Corbie Mitleid, Reverend (USA) Category: Angel Reader. 5 stars
- Corbie Mitleid, Reverend (USA) Category: Life-Coach Psychic. 5 stars
- Craig Webb (USA) Category: Dream Interpreter. 4 stars
- Crimson Kitty (USA) Category: Tarot Reader. 4 stars
- Crista Sokolow (USA) Category: Healer. 4 stars

D

- Damian Nordmann (USA) Category: Dream Interpreter. 4 stars
- Daniel Dowd (USA) Category: Astrologer. 4 stars
- Darlene Lancer, JD (USA) Category: Dream Interpreter. 5 stars
- Darlene Lancer, JD (USA) Category: Dream Interpreter. 5 stars
- Dave Schrader (USA) Category: Best Paranormal Radio Show Hosts in the US. 4 stars
- Dave Schrader (USA) Category: Paranormal Researcher. 4 stars

- Dave Young (USA) Category: Ghost Hunter. 5 stars
- Dave Young (USA) Category: Paranormal Researcher. 4 stars
- Daved Beck (USA) Category: Medium. 5 stars
- Daved Beck (USA) Category: Psychic. 5 stars
- David Beck (USA) Category: Life-Coach Psychic. 4 stars
- David Lawrence Palmer (USA) Category: Astrologer. 4 stars
- Dawn Champine (USA) Category: Feng Shui practitioner. 4 stars
- Dawn Short (USA) Category: Psychic. 4 stars
- DC Love (USA) Category: Healer. 4 stars
- DC Love (USA) Category: Pet Psychic/Animal Communicator. 4 stars
- Dean Kraft (USA) Category: Healer. 5 stars
- Deb McBride (USA) Category: Astrologer. 4 stars
- Deborah Leblanc (USA) Category: Medium. 4 stars
- Debra Clement (USA) Category: Astrologer. 5 stars
- Debra Davies (USA) Category: Reiki Practitioner. 5 stars
- Deidre Madsen (USA) Category: Medium. 4 stars
- Dena Flanagan (USA) Category: Healer. 4 stars
- Dena Flanagan (USA) Category: Medium. 4 stars
- Denise Bennett (USA) Category: Angel Reader. 5 stars
- Diane Hiller (USA) Category: Life-Coach Psychic. 5 stars
- Diane Hiller (USA) Category: Medium. 5 stars
- Diane Hiller (USA) Category: Psychic. 5 stars
- Diane Hiller (USA) Category: Feng Shui practitioner. 5 stars
- Diane Williams (USA) Category: Healer. 5 stars
- Diane Williams (USA) Category: Tarot Reader. 4 stars
- Dina Vitantonio (USA) Category: Healer. 4 stars
- Djuna Davitashvili (Russia)
- Dolores Cannon (USA) Category: Best Metaphysical Teacher. 5 stars
- Dolores Krieger, RN, Ph.D. (USA) Category: Healer. 5 stars
- Dolores Krieger, RN, Ph.D. (USA) Category: Healer. 5 stars
- Doreen Virtue (USA) Category: Angel Reader. 5 stars

- Doreen Virtue (USA) Category: Psychic. 5 stars
- Dorothy Allyson (USA) Category: Psychic. 4 stars
- Doyle Ward (USA) Category: Life-Coach Psychic. 5 stars
- Doyle Ward (USA) Category: Psychic. 5 stars

E

- Edward Shanahan (USA) Category: Palmist. 4 stars
- Elisa Medhus (USA) Category: Healer. 4 stars
- Elisjah Anderzen (USA) Category: Healer. 4 stars
- Elizabeth Barnett (USA) Category: Angel Reader. 5 stars
- Elizabeth Baron (USA) Category: Psychic. 4 stars
- Elizabeth Joyce (USA) Category: Psychic. 5 stars
- Eric Linter (USA) Category: Astrologer. 5 stars

F

- Faith McInerney (USA) Category: Astrologer. 4 stars
- 4 stars Faye Drummond (USA) Category: Reiki Practitioner. 5 stars
- Frank Andrews (USA) Category: Psychic. 4 stars
- Frank Andrews (USA) Category: Tarot Reader. 5 stars

G

- Gary Wimmer (USA) Category: Psychic. 4 stars
- George Noory (USA) (USA) Category: Best Paranormal Radio Show Hosts in the US. 5 stars
- George Noory (USA) Category: Paranormal Researcher. 5 stars
- Ginger Quinlan (USA) Category: Angel Reader. 4 stars
- Ginny Ciszek (USA) Category: Spirit Artist. 4 stars
- Gliselda Amarillas-Ramirez (USA) Category: Angel Reader. 4 stars
- Grant Wilson (USA) Category: Ghost Hunter. 5 stars
- Grant Wilson: (USA) Category: Paranormal Researcher. 4 stars

- Greta Alexander (USA) Category: Psychic. 5 stars

H

- Heather Valentine (USA) Category: Angel Reader. 4 stars
- Heidi Jaffe (USA) Category: Medium. 4 stars
- Helene Frisch (USA) Category: Psychic. 4 stars

I

- Irene Hope Burke (USA) Category: Psychic. 5 stars
- Iris Saltzman (USA) Category: Astrologer. 4 stars
- Issam Nemeh, MD (USA) Category: Healer. 5 stars

J

- Jack Gray (USA) Category: Healer. 5 stars
- Jacque McPherson (USA) Category: Angel Reader. 4 stars
- Jake Samoyedny (USA) Category: Medium. 5 stars
- James Van Praagh (USA) Category: Psychic. 5 stars
- Jamie Butler (USA) Category: Medium. 5 stars
- Jamie Butler (USA) Category: Psychic. 4 stars
- Jamie Clark (USA) Category: Psychic. 4 stars
- Jan Drake Bakke (USA) Category: Psychic. 4 stars
- Jane Teresa Anderson (USA) Category: Dream Interpreter. 5 stars
- Janet Bowerman (USA Category: Healer. 4 stars
- Janette Kaye (USA) Category: Spirit Artist. 5 stars
- Janette Oakman (USA) Category: Spirit Artist. 4 stars
- Janine Regan Sinclair (USA) Category: Psychic. 4 stars
- Janine Regan Sinclair (USA) Category: Healer. 4 stars
- Jean Salch (USA) Category: Healer. 4 stars
- Jeannie Lindheim (USA) Category: Pet Psychic/Animal Communicator. 4 stars
- Jeannine Bakriges (USA) Category: Medium. 4 stars
- Jeannine G Wand (USA) Category: Healer. 4 stars

- Jen Prothero (USA) Category: Angel Reader. 4 stars
- Jennifer Shackford (USA) Category: Angel Reader. 5 stars
- Jennifer Shackford (USA) Category: Psychic. 4 stars
- Jennifer Shaffer (USA) Category: Healer. 4 stars
- Jennifer Wallens (USA) Categories: Medium. Psychic, Spirit Artist. Pet Psychic/Animal Communicator. 5 stars
- Jennifer Wallens (USA) Category: Paranormal Researcher. 5 stars
- Jennifer Wallens (USA) Category: Pet Psychic/Animal Communicator. 5 stars
- Jennifer Wallens (USA) Category: Spirit Artist. 5 stars
- Jeri Ryan (USA) Category: Pet Psychic/Animal Communicator. 5 stars
- Jessica Lanyadoo (USA) Category: Astrologer. 4 stars
- Jessicca Cannon Haas (USA) Category: Medium. 5 stars
- Jethro Smith (USA) Category: Best Paranormal Radio Show Hosts in the US. 5 stars
- Jethro Smith (USA) Category: Healer. 4 stars
- Jethro Smith (USA) Category: Medium. 5 stars
- Jethro Smith (USA) Category: Paranormal Researcher. 5 stars
- Jethro Smith (USA) Category: Pet Psychic/Animal Communicator. 4 stars
- Jethro Smith (USA) Category: Tarot Reader. 5 stars
- Jill Beiler (USA) Category: Medium. 4 stars
- Joan Bunyan (USA) Category: Psychic. 4 stars
- Joan Ranquet (USA) Category: Pet Psychic and Animal Communicator. 5 stars
- Joanne Gerber (USA) Category: Psychic. 4 stars
- Joe Nicols (USA) Category: Palmist. 4 stars
- Johanna Morgan, MA, CHT (USA) Category: Healer. 5 stars
- John Cappello (USA) Category: Medium. 5 stars
- John Cappello (USA) Category: Psychic. 5 stars
- John Harricharan (USA) Category: Psychic. 5 stars
- John Seed Bearer (USA) Category: Dream Interpreter. 4 stars
- Joseph Shiel (USA) Category: Spirit Artist. 4 stars

- Joy Rilling (USA) Category: Tarot Reader. 4 stars
- Joyce Keller (USA) Category: Psychic. 5 stars
- Joyce Markwick (USA) Category: Spirit Artist. 4 stars
- Judy Hevenly (USA) Category: Psychic. 4 stars
- Judy Kelly (USA) Category: Reiki Practitioner. 5 stars
- Julie Lynn Rogers (USA) Category: Angel Reader. 4 stars

K

- Karen Page (USA) Category: Psychic. 5 stars
- Karen Thorne (USA) Category: Astrologer. 4 stars
- Karen Wrigley (USA) Category: Pet Psychic and Animal Communicator. 4 stars
- Karen Wrigley (USA) Category: Pet Psychic/Animal Communicator. 5 stars
- Karina Voroshilova (USA) Category: Medium. 5 stars
- Karina Voroshilova (USA) Category: Psychic. 4 stars
- Karina Voroshilova (USA) Category: Tarot Reader. 4 stars
- Katherine Glass (USA) Category: Medium. 5 stars
- Kathlyn Rhea. (USA) Category: Psychic. 5 stars
- Kathryn Samuelson (USA) Category: Angel Reader. 4 stars
- Kay Jacobs (USA) Category: Healer. 4 stars
- Keli Michaels (USA) Category: Psychic. 4 stars
- Kelley Hunter, PH.D. (Virgin Islands) Category: Astrologer. 4 stars
- Kelly Coulter (USA) Category: Healer. 4 stars
- Kelly Coulter (USA) Category: Psychic. 4 stars
- Khatie Lipinski (USA) Category: Reiki Practitioner. 5 stars
- Kim Russo (USA) Category: Medium. 5 stars
- Kim Russo (USA) Category: Paranormal Researcher. 5 stars
- Kim Russo (USA) Category: Psychic. 5 stars
- Kimberly Ward (USA) Category: Psychic. 5 stars
- Kimberly Ward, Reverend (USA) Category: Life-Coach Psychic. 5 stars

- Krishnendu Chakraborty, Ph.D. (India/Inde) Category: Astrologer. 4 stars
- Kristin Thompson (USA) Category: Pet Psychic/Animal Communicator. 4 stars
- Kristopher Kotch (USA) Category: Dream Interpreter. 4 stars
- Krzysztof "Kris" Chmielewski (USA) Category: Psychic. 4 stars
- Krzysztof "Kris" Chmielewski (USA) Category: Tarot Reader. 5 stars

L

- Larry Sang (USA) Category: Feng Shui practitioner. 5 stars
- Laura Alden Kamm (USA) Category: Healer. 4 stars
- Laura Colavito-Agosta (USA) Category: Tarot Reader. 4 stars
- Laura Lyn (USA) Category: Angel Reader. 5 stars
- Laura Mendelsohn (USA) Category: Psychic. 5 stars
- Lauri Quinn Loewenberg (USA) Category: Dream Interpreter. 5 stars
- Lee Papa (USA) Category: Healer. 4 stars
- Leila Esber (USA) (USA) Category: Dream Interpreter. 4 stars
- Leslie Shapiro (USA) Category: Ghost Hunter. 5 stars
- Leslie Shapiro (USA) Category: Paranormal Researcher. 4 stars
- Linda Black (USA) Category: Astrologer. 4 stars
- Linda Carney (USA) Category: Life-Coach Psychic. 5 stars
- Linda Lauren (USA) Category: Psychic. 5 stars
- Linda Messerman (USA) Category: Pet Psychic/Animal Communicator. 5 stars
- Linda Salvin, Ph.D. (USA) Category: Psychic. 4 stars
- Linda Shandra (USA) Category: Dream Interpreter. 4 stars
- Lisa Atkinson (USA) Category: Angel Reader. 4 stars
- Lisa Beachy (USA) Category: Angel Reader. 4 stars
- Lisa Campion (USA) Category: Healer. 5 stars

- Lisa Nevot (USA) Category: Spirit Artist. 5 stars
- Lisa Williams (USA) Category: Psychic. 5 stars
- Lisa Williams (USA) Category: Medium. 5 stars
- Litany Burns (USA) Category: Psychic. 5 stars
- Loretta Standley, Dr. (USA) Category: Astrologer. 4 stars
- Lori Coviello (USA) Category: Healer. 4 stars
- Lori Green Connell (USA) Category: Healer. 4 stars
- Lori Karras (USA) Category: Psychic. 4 stars
- Lori Marshall (USA) Category: Spirit Artist. 5 stars
- Lorie Johnson (USA) Category: Healer. 4 stars
- Lorie Johnson (USA) Category: Pet Psychic/Animal Communicator. 4 stars
- Lorie Johnson (USA) Category: Psychic. 5 stars
- Lorie Johnson (USA) Category: Medium. 4 stars
- Lorraine Lush (USA) Category: Medium. 4 stars
- Lorraine Lush (USA) Category: Psychic. 4 stars
- Lorraine Roe (USA) Category: Psychic 5 stars
- Lorraine Roe (USA) Category: Medium. 5 stars
- Lorraine Turner (USA) Category: Pet Psychic/Animal Communicator. 4 stars
- Lorraine Turner (USA) Category: Spirit Artist. 4 stars
- Lydia Clar (USA) Category: Psychic. 4 stars
- Lydia Hiby (USA) Category: Pet Psychic/Animal Communicator. 5 stars
- Lyle Sharman (USA) Category: Paranormal Researcher. 4 stars
- Lynn Boggess (USA) Category: Reiki Practitioner. 5 stars
- Lynsi Wood (USA) Category: Tarot Reader. 4 stars

M

- Magdalena Gjesvold (USA) Category: Medium. 5 stars
- Mandy Carr (USA) Category: Pet Psychic and Animal Communicator. 5 stars
- Mandy Carr (USA) Category: Pet Psychic/Animal Communicator. 5 stars
- Maria Jensen (USA) Category: Angel Reader. 4 stars

- Maria Shaw-Lawson (USA) Category: Numerologist. 5 stars
- Mariana Cooper (USA) Category: Angel Reader. 4 stars
- Mark Seltman (USA) Category: Palmist. 5 stars
- Marla Phillips (USA) Category: Psychic. 4 stars
- Martha Piesco Hoff (USA) Category: Healer. 5 stars
- Martha Williams (USA) Category: Pet Psychic/Animal Communicator. 5 stars
- Mary Ann Kotch (USA) Category: Dream Interpreter. 4 stars
- Mary Ennis (USA) Category: Psychic. 5 stars
- Mary Marshall (USA)
- Mary Strauss (USA) Category: Angel Reader. 4 stars
- Mary T. Browne (USA) Category: Psychic. 5 stars
- Master Yau (USA) Category: Feng Shui practitioner. 4 stars
- Matthew Brandau (USA) Category: Medium. 4 stars
- Psychic/Animal Communicator. 4 stars
- Maxson J. McDowell PhD, LMSW, LP (USA) Category: Dream Interpreter. 4 stars
- Maxson J. McDowell PhD, LMSW, LP (USA) Category: Dream Interpreter. 4 stars
- Maya Britan (USA) Category: Psychic. 4 stars
- Melissa Bacelar (USA) Category: Pet Psychic/Animal Communicator. 4 stars
- Melissa Berman (USA) Category: Psychic. 5 stars
- Melissa Berman (USA) Category: Medium. 5 stars
- Melissa Berman (USA) Category: Life-Coach Psychic. 5 stars
- Melissa Stamps (USA) Category: Feng Shui practitioner. 4 stars
- Melissa Stamps (USA) Category: Life-Coach Psychic. 5 stars
- Melissa Stamps (USA) Category: Psychic. 5 stars
- Michael and Marti Parry (USA) Category: Spirit Artist. 4 stars
- Michael Lutin (USA) Category: Astrologer. 4 stars
- Michelle Whitedove (USA) Category: Psychic. 5 stars
- Michelle Whitedove (USA) Category: Medium. 5 stars

- Michelle Whitedove (USA) Category: Angel Reader. 5 stars
- Michelle Sheahan (USA) Category: Reiki Practitioner. 5 stars
- Micki Dahne (USA) Category: Psychic. 5 stars
- Mychael Shane, Rev. (USA) Category: Physical medium. 4 stars

N

- Nadia Shapiro (USA) Category: Medium. 4 stars
- Nadia Starella (USA) Category: Angel Reader. 5 stars
- Nancine Meyer (USA) Category: Angel Reader. 4 stars
- Nancy Christie Johansen (USA) Category: Angel Reader. 4 stars
- Nancy Myer (USA) Category: Psychic. 4 stars
- Nancy Wagaman, MA (USA) Category: Dream Interpreter. 4 stars
- Nicki Bonfilio (USA) Category: Psychic. 4 stars
- Nicolas David Ngan (USA) Category: Numerologist. 4 stars
- Noelle Garneau (USA) Category: Angel Reader. 5 stars
- Noelle Garneau (USA) Category: Psychic. 5 stars
- Noreen Renier (USA) Category: Psychic. 4 stars

O

- Oktobre Taylor (USA) Category: Healer. 4 stars

P

- Pam Case (USA) Category: Pet Psychic/Animal Communicator. 5 stars
- Pam Coronado (USA) Category: Psychic. 4 stars
- Pam Ragland (USA) Category: Healer. 5 stars
- Pamela Beaty, Reverend (USA) Category: Life-Coach Psychic. 5 stars
- Patrice Cole (USA) Category: Astrologer. 5 stars

- Patrice Cole (USA) Category: Intuitive Entertainer. 5 stars
- Patrice Cole (USA) Category: Numerologist. 5 stars
- Patricia Masters (USA) Category: Psychic. 4 stars
- Patricia Mischell (USA) Category: Psychic. 5 stars
- Patricia Naffki (USA) Category: Reiki Practitioner. 5 stars
- Patricia Richards (USA) Category: Pet Psychic/Animal Communicator. 4 stars
- Patti Negri (USA) Categories: Medium. Psychic, Tarot Reader, Witch. 5 stars
- Patti Negri (USA) Category: Best Paranormal Radio Show Hosts in the US. 5 stars
- Patti Negri (USA) Category: Medium. 5 stars
- Patti Negri (USA) Category: Paranormal Researcher. 5 stars
- Patti Negri (USA) Category: Tarot Reader. 5 stars
- Patti Negri (USA) Category: White magic. 5 stars
- Patti Negri (USA) Category: Witchcraft and Magick. 5 stars
- Patti Negri: (USA) Category: Intuitive Entertainer. 5 stars
- Peg Jones (USA) Category: Psychic. 4 stars
- Penelope Smith (USA) Category: Pet Psychic/Animal Communicator. 5 stars
- PennyC (USA) Category: Angel Reader. 5 stars
- PennyC. (USA) Category: Life-Coach Psychic. 5 stars
- Phil Jordan (USA) Category: Psychic Detective. 5 stars

R

- Rachel Marie (USA) Category: Medium. 4 stars
- Rachel Marie (USA) Category: Pet Psychic/Animal Communicator. 4 stars
- Rachel Marie (USA) Category: Psychic. 4 stars
- Rae Ramsey (USA) Category: Pet Psychic/Animal Communicator. 4 stars
- Ray Schmidt (USA) Category: Paranormal Researcher. 4 stars

- Rick Borutta (USA) Category: Astrologer. 4 stars
- Rick Hayes (USA) Category: Medium. 5 stars
- Rita Berkowitz (USA) Category: Spirit Artist. 5 stars
- Rita Berkowitz (USA) Category: Medium. 5 stars
- Robert Rodriguez (USA) Category: Healer. 4 stars
- Robert Rodriguez (USA) Category: Psychic. 5 stars
- Robert Rodriguez (USA) Category: Tarot Reader. 4 stars
- Robin (USA) Category: Angel Reader. 4 stars
- Robyne Marie, Reverend (USA) Category: Spirit Photographer/Scrying Medium. 5 stars
- Roger Laborde (USA) Category: Healer. 5 stars
- Roger Nobles (USA) (Non-Traditional/At distance) Category: Reiki Practitioner. 5 stars
- Roger Nobles (USA) Category: Dream Interpreter. 4 stars
- Roger Nobles (USA) Category: Healer. 4 stars
- Rosalind Coleman (USA) Category: Spirit Artist. 5 stars
- Rosalyn Bruyere, DD (USA) Category: Healer. 4 stars
- Rosalyn Bruyere, DD (USA) Category: Healer. 5 stars
- Rose Ann Schwab, Ph.D. (USA) Category: Angel Reader. 5 stars
- Rosemary Altea (USA) Category: Psychic. 4 stars
- Ross J. Miller USA) Category: Dream Interpreter. 4 stars
- Roxanne Elizabeth Useman (USA) Category: Medium. 5 stars
- Roxanne Elizabeth Useman (USA) Category: Psychic. 4 stars
- Ruth Larkin (USA) Category: Healer. 5 stars
- Ruth Larkin (USA) Category: Reiki Practitioner. 5 stars

S

- Sally Brustowicz (USA) Category: Psychic. 4 stars
- Samanta Hawes (USA) Category: Ghost Hunter. 5 stars
- Samantha Hall (USA) Category: Pet Psychic/Animal Communicator. 4 stars
- Samantha Hawes (USA) Category: Paranormal Researcher. 4 stars

- Sandra Helton. (USA) Category: Astrologer. 4 stars
- Sandra Nemet (USA) Category: Psychic. 4 stars
- Sandra Nemet (USA) Category: Medium. 4 stars
- Sarah West (USA) Category: Healer. 5 stars
- Sasha Fenton (UK/Angleterre) Category: Astrologer. 4 stars
- Shannon Leischner (USA) Category: Angel Reader. 5 stars
- Shannon Leischner (USA) Category: Life-Coach Psychic. 5 stars
- Shannon Leischner (USA) Category: Psychic. 5 stars
- Sharon Kissane (USA) Category: Psychic. 4 stars
- Sharon Pugh (USA) Category: Psychic. 4 stars
- Sharon Warner (USA) Category: Pet Psychic/Animal Communicator. 4 stars
- Shellee Halle (USA) Category: Psychic Detective. 5 stars
- Sherie Hurd Roufusse (Canada/USA) Categories: Psychic and medium. 5 stars
- Sherie Hurd Roufusse (Canada/USA) Category: Spirit Photographer/Scrying Medium. 4 stars
- Sindi Somers (USA) Category: Pet Psychic/Animal Communicator. 4 stars
- Solana (USA) Category: Healer. 4 stars
- Solana (USA) Category: Pet Psychic/Animal Communicator. 4 stars
- Sonya Fitzpatrick (USA) Category: Pet Psychic and Animal Communicator. 4 stars
- Sonya Fitzpatrick (USA) Category: Pet Psychic/Animal Communicator. 5 stars
- Stacey Wolf-James (USA) Category: Psychic. 5 stars
- Stan Kestral (USA) Category: Pet Psychic/Animal Communicator. 4 stars
- Stephen Robinson (USA) Category: Psychic. 4 stars
- Steve Blaze (USA) Category: Ghost Hunter. 5 stars
- Steve Blaze (USA) Category: Paranormal Researcher. 4 stars
- Steven D. Farmer, MD (USA) Category: Pet Psychic/Animal Communicator. 4 stars
- Steven Weiss, MD (USA) Category: Healer. 5 stars

- Sue Hopple (USA) Category: Pet Psychic/Animal Communicator. 4 stars
- Sue Manley (USA) Category: Pet Psychic/Animal Communicator. 4 stars
- Sue Pike (USA) Category: Pet Psychic/Animal Communicator. 4 stars
- Sue Raye (USA) Category: Psychic. 4 stars
- Sue Reeder (USA) Category: Spirit Artist. 4 stars
- Sunhee Park (USA) Category: Psychics. 5 stars
- Susan Averre (USA) Category: Spirit Artist. 4 stars
- Susan Deren (USA) Category: Pet Psychic/Animal Communicator. 4 stars
- Susannah Spanton (USA) Category: Psychic. 5 stars
- Suzane Grace (USA) Category: Psychic. 5 stars
- Suzane Grace (USA) Category: Medium. 5 stars
- Suzanne Grace (USA) Category: Angel Reader. 5 stars
- Suzanne Grace (USA) Category: Life-Coach Psychic. 5 stars

T

- Tara Viosca Mead (USA) Category: Spirit Photographer/Scrying Medium. 5 stars
- Tarah Harper (USA) Category: Dream Interpreter. 5 stars
- Tarah Harper (USA) Category: Healer. 5 stars
- Tarah Harper (USA) Category: Psychic. 4 stars
- Tereza Jantz (USA) Category: Reiki Practitioner. 5 stars
- Terry and Linda Jamison (USA) Category: Psychic. 4 stars
- Terry Nazon (USA) Category: Astrologer. 4 stars
- Theresa Caputo (USA) Category: Psychic. 4 stars
- Thomas John (USA) Category: Psychic. 4 stars
- Tiffany Powers (USA) Category: Medium. 5 stars
- Tina Carey (USA) Category: Tarot Reader. 4 stars
- Tina Saelee (USA/Thailand) Category: Healer. 4 stars
- Tracy Lee Nash (USA) Category: Psychic. 5 stars
- Trilby Johnson (USA) Category: Healer. 4 stars

V

- Vicki Monroe (USA) Category: Medium. 5 stars
- Vickie Gay (USA) Categories: Psychic and medium. 5 stars
- Virginia Bell (USA) Category: Astrologer. 4 stars
- Vivian Carol (USA) Category: Astrologer. 4 stars

W

- Willian Rand (USA) Category: Reiki Practitioner. 5 stars

Y

- Yolanda Billings (USA): Category: Tarot Reader. 5 stars

*** *** ***

Best Spiritual Guides in the United States

Reverend Diane Davis

Reverend Davis was the only spiritual guide from the United States who appear on the vote list of the New York International Vote 2014-2015.

Best Metaphysical Teachers in the United States

- **American lightworkers who are on the list of Top 10 best metaphysical teachers in the world:**
- In 6th Place:
- Doreen Virtue
- In 7th Place:
- Dolores Cannon
- In 8th Place:
- Lisa Williams
- In 9th Place:
- Reverend Diane Davis

- **From the Top 15 best metaphysical teachers in the world:**
- **In 11th Place:**
- Anna Robles Simon

Dolores Cannon (USA). Lisa Willians (USA).

Doreen Virtue (USA). Rev. Diane Davis (USA).

Anna Robles Simon (USA).

LIGHTWORKERS OF THE YEAR

Lightworker of the year award is an extremely important award, granted to lightworkers who are considered by our community and peers as "role model". They are the practitioners who set the highest moral, ethical and professional standards. Those are the practitioners who brought credibility, respect, dignity, and honor to the profession. They are the ones who care, the loving and efficient spiritual guides who walk with you and extra mile. The trustworthy, the honorable and simply put "the ones who deliver the goods." In the opinion of New York International Vote, those who are nominated to this great honor are as important as those who have captured the first rank, the first place in any category. In fact, in many instances, they are considered more important and more efficient than those who made the "Top 5 List".Because they have demonstrated excellence, commitment to their clients, and an absolute integrity, which are not categorically the "traits" of the big winners in this vote.

Men's category: Lightworkers of the Year

Nominations in alphabetical order

C
Chip Coffey
Daved Peck
Doyle Ward
John Holland
Doyle Ward (USA)

Doyle Ward

Women's category: Lightworkers of the Year

Voted in alphabetical order.

A
Allison Hayes
Anita Rosenberg

C
Chinhee Park
Concetta Bertoldi

D
Diane Hiller
Dolores Krieger, RN, Ph.D.
Doreen Virtue

J
Jennifer Wallens
Jessicca Haas

K
Keli Michaels
Kim Russo
Kimberly Ward

L
Lisa Campion
Lorraine Roe

M
Michelle Whitedove
Micki Dahne

P
Patrice Cole
Patti Negri

R
Rosalyn Bruyere, DD

S
Sunhee Park/Chinhee Park
Suzanne Grace

T
Tracy Lee Nash

V
Vicky Gay

Y
Yolanda Billings (USA)

In international rank order:

From left to right: Patti Negri, Tracy Lee Nash.

Jennifer Wallens, Yolanda Billings.

- **Top Five:**
- **In 1st Place:**

- Patti Negri
- **In 2nd Place:**
- Tracy Lee Nash
- **In 3rd Place:**
- Jennifer Wallens
- **In 4th Place:**
- Yolanda Billings

*** *** ***

WOMAN OF THE YEAR 2014

This is an extremely important award, for it requires more than extraordinary supernatural gifts to be recognized as Woman of the Year. This award is granted to a person whose accomplishments and services to the world's community are unsurpassed on so many levels. Woman of the Year is a role model in the true sense. Her importance transcends the frontiers of success, fame and authority of the occult, paranormal and metaphysical realm.

Such accomplishments encompass a multitude of magnificent deeds, services and contributions to humanity, such as, to name a few:

1-Creation of a center of learning (An academy, a school, a center of training, a spiritual retreat).

2-Development of guidance programs.

3-Distinguished teaching at reputable institutions.

4-Documented humanitarian services which changed the life of people.

5-Authorship (Writing books) which enlightened the seekers of knowledge, and truth.

6-Extraordinary discoveries in the field. So on.

American women who have shaped and defined the world of lightworkers.
The most influential women in the business. When these women talk, everybody listens.

In alphabetical order:

A
Allison Hayes "The Rock Girl"

C
Carol Gurney

D
Doreen Virtue

G
Gretta Alexander

J
Jennifer Wallens
Joan Ranquet

L
Liane Buck
Lisa Campion
Lydia Hiby

M
Michelle Whitedove
Micki Dahne

P
Patrice Cole
Patti Negri
Penelope Smith

S

Shay Paker
Sunhee Park and Chinhee Park

T
Tracy Lee Nash

V
Vickie Gay

From left to right: Patti Negri. Jennifer Wallens.

Patrice Cole. Vickie Gay.

Tracy Lee Nash. Sunhee Park and Chinhee Park.

Gretta Alexander. Doreen Virtue.

Joan Ranquet. Carol Gurney.

Lydia Hiby. Lisa Campion.

Michelle Whitedove. Alison Hayes the Rock Girl.

LIGHTWORKERS' WORLD HALL OF FAME

Every year, the general public around the world submits names of lightworkers who deserve to be inducted into the Lightworkers' World Hall of Fame. There are over 856,500 practitioners on the planet, but few shine brighter than the sun. Those are the lightworkers known for their integrity, commitment, truth, accuracy, and services rendered to our communities around the globe. The tradition continues, and as you have done in the past, submit up to 5 names you honestly believe they deserve to receive the "Life Achievement Award", and be added to the roster of "Lightworkers' World Hall of Fame." Submit nominations to Mr. M. de Lafayette at delafayette6@aol.com

LIGHTWORKERS LIFE ACHIEVEMENT AWARD

LIGHTWORKERS' WORLD HALL OF FAME

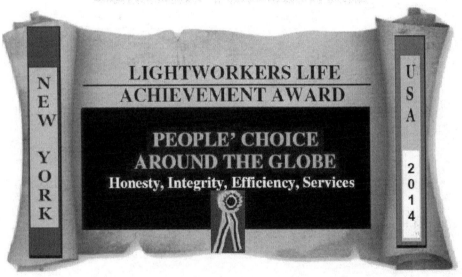

Lightworkers World Hall Of Fame:

Names submitted for consideration:
Irene Hope Burke
Joy Rilling
Lorraine Turner
Samantha Hall
Sherie Hurd Roufosse
Hall Of Fame New Inductees (2014)
Concetta Bertoldi
Vickie Gay

BEST MEDIUMS
IN THE WORLD

AMERICAN MEDIUMS WHO MADE THE LIST OF THE BEST MEDIUMS IN THE WORLD

By alphabetical order, from the international roster.

A

- Adam Bernstein (USA)
- Agnes Obrzanowska (USA)
- Alex Treglazoff (USA)
- Amy Diggins (USA)
- Angela Bixby (USA)
- Angela Kruszka (USA)
- Anthony Morgann (USA)
- Astrid Stromberg (USA)
- Aurora Rose aka Stephanie Stinnett (USA)

B

- B. Anne Gehman, Reverend (USA)
- Barbara Almond (USA)
- Barbara DeLong (USA)
- Belinda Bentley (USA)
- Bella Mason (USA)
- Belle Salisbury (USA)
- Bonnie Albers (USA)
- Bree Peltier (USA)

C

- Carrie-Anne Hartley Silkowski (USA)
- Cassandra Larsen (USA)
- Catherine Birkhimer (USA)
- Catherine Dougherty (USA)
- Cathie Bradshaw (USA)
- Cathy Towle (USA)
- Charlene Hicks (USA)
- Christina Nelson (USA)
- Cindy Greene (USA)
- Claire Braddock (USA)

- Concetta Bertoldi (USA)

D

- Daved Beck (USA)
- Dawn Bothie (USA)
- Dawn Mystic Haven (USA)
- DC Love (USA)
- Debra Leblanc (USA)
- Deidre Madsen (USA)
- Dena Flanagan (USA)
- Diane Hiller (USA)
- Diane Williams (USA)
- Dianne Winbauer (USA)
- Donna McGrath (USA)

E

- Eileen Boettcher (USA)
- Elisjah Anderzen (USA)
- Eric Glyn (USA)

F

- Feebee McIntyre (USA)

G

- Gemini Rose (USA)
- Georgia Marantos (USA)
- Greg Kehn (USA)

H

- Heidi Jaffe (USA)
- Hillary Freitas (USA)
- Hoyt Robinette (USA)

I

- Irene Hope Burke (USA)
- Isabelle Dawes (USA)

J

- Jake Samoyedny (USA)
- Jamie Butler (USA)
- Jeanne Clock (USA)
- Jeannine Bakriges (USA)
- Jen Queen (USA)
- Jennifer Shackford (USA)
- Jennifer Wallens (USA)
- Jessicca Cannon Haas (USA)
- Jethro Smith (USA)
- Jill Beiler (USA)
- John Cappello (USA)
- Jonna Kay Carlson (USA)
- Joshua John (USA)
- Joyce Markwick (USA)

K

- Karen Cote (USA)
- Karina Voroshilova (USA)
- Karleen Heller (USA)
- Katherine Glass (USA)
- Kim Russo (USA)
- Kimberley Smith (USA)
- Kristen Leona (USA)

L

- Linda Jolley (USA)
- Lisa Bousson (USA)
- Lisa Williams (USA)
- Lorie Johnson (USA)
- Lorraine Lush (USA)
- Lorraine Roe (USA)

- Lynn Bleasdale (USA)

M

- Magdalena Gjesvold (USA)
- Mandy Thompson (USA)
- Marisa Ryan (USA)
- Matthew Brandau (USA)
- Matthew Smith (USA)
- Medium Irene (USA)
- Melissa Berman (USA)

N

- Nadia Shapiro (USA)
- Nodira Standard (USA)
- Noemia Walaska (USA)

O

- Oktobre Taylor (USA)

P

- Patricia O'Boyle, Reverend (USA)
- Patrick De Haan (USA)
- Patti Negri (USA)

R

- Rachel Marie (USA)
- Rachel S. Kohler (USA)
- Renee Richards (USA)
- Richard Schoeller (USA)
- Rick Hayes (USA)
- Rita Berkowitz (USA)
- Robert Rodriguez (USA)
- Roxanne Elizabeth Usleman (USA)

- Ruth Larkin (USA)
- Ryan Smith (USA)

S

- Samantha McGovern (USA)
- Sammie Jo Huffstetler (USA)
- Sandra Nemet (USA)
- Sarah McCoy (USA)
- Sarina St. John (USA)
- Saundra Greene (USA)
- Shanon Corkins (USA)
- Shereece Davison (USA)
- Sherie Hurd Roufosse (USA)
- Simone Key (UK/USA)
- Sondra Sneed (USA)
- Stevie Pierce (USA)
- Susan Sanderford (USA)
- Susie Grimett (USA)
- Suzanne Grace (USA)

T

- Terri Daniel (USA)
- Thomas John (USA)
- Tiffany Powers (USA)
- Timitha Bryan (USA)
- Tina Carey (USA)
- Tracy Lee Nash (USA)
- Trish Woods (USA)

U

- Ursula Kalin (USA)

V

- Venus Andrecht (USA)
- Vicki Monroe (USA)

- Vickie Gay (USA)

- **W**
- Wendy Reinli (USA)

*** *** ***

Americans who made the list of the world's best mediums in international rank order.

TOP 5 MEDIUMS IN THE WORLD:
- **In 1st Place :**
- Patti Negri
- Jennifer Wallens
- **In 3rd Place:**
- Vickie Gay
- **In 4th Place:**
- Tracy Lee Nash

From left to Right: Patti Negri. Jennifer Wallens.

51

Vickie Gay. Tracy Lee Nash.

TOP 10 MEDIUMS IN THE WORLD : ⭐⭐⭐⭐⭐
- **In 8th Place:**
- Suzanne Grace
- **In 9th Place:**
- Diane Hiller
- **In 10th Place:**
- Jessicca Cannon Haas

Suzanne Grace. Diane Hiller.

Jessicca Cannon Haas.

TOP 15 MEDIUMS IN THE WORLD :
- **In 11th Place:**
- John Cappello

John Cappello.

TOP 20 MEDIUMS IN THE WORLD :
- **In 19th Place:**
- Roxanne Elizabeth Usleman
- **In 20th Place:**
- Lorraine Roe

Roxanne Elizabeth Usleman. Lorraine Roe.

TOP 25 MEDIUMS IN THE WORLD : ★★★★★
- **In 21st Place:**
- Amy Diggins
- **In 23rd Place:**
- B. Anne Gehman, Reverend
- **In 24th Place:**
- Lisa Williams

Amy Diggins. B. Anne Gehman.

Lisa Williams.

TOP 30 MEDIUMS IN THE WORLD : ★★★★★
- **In 27th Place**
- Rita Berkowitz
- **In 28th Place:**
- Concetta Bertoldi
- **In 29th Place**
- Ruth Larkin
- **In 30th Place:**
- Melissa Berman

Rita Berkowitz. Concetta Bertoldi.

Ruth Larkin. Melissa Berman.

TOP 35 MEDIUMS IN THE WORLD :

- **In 33rd Place:**
- Jake Samoyedny
- **In 34th Place:**
- Kim Russo
- **In 35th Place:**
- Jethro Smith

Jake Samoyedny. Kim Rousso.

Jethro Smith.

TOP 40 MEDIUMS IN THE WORLD :

- **In 37th Place:**
- Jamie Butler
- **In 38th Place:**
- Cathy Towle
- **In 40th Place:**
- Rick Hayes

Vicki Monroe. Lorie Johnson.

Cathy Towle.

Rick Hayes.. Jamie Butler.

TOP 45 MEDIUMS IN THE WORLD :
- **In 41th Place:**
- Vicki Monroe
- **In 43rd Place:**
- Lorie Johnson

TOP 50 MEDIUMS IN THE WORLD :
- **In 47th Place:**
- Heidi Jaffe
- **In 49th Place:**
- Daved Beck

TOP 55 MEDIUMS IN THE WORLD :
- **In 53rd Place:**
- Lorraine Lush
- **In 54th Place:**
- Dena Flanagan
- Karina Voroshilova

TOP 65 MEDIUMS IN THE WORLD :
- **In 62nd Place:**
- Magdalena Gjesvold
- **In 63rd Place:**
- Tiffany Powers
- **In 65th Place:**

- Katherine Glass

TOP 70 MEDIUMS IN THE WORLD : ⭐⭐⭐
- **In 70th Place:**
- Belle Salisbury

TOP 75 MEDIUMS IN THE WORLD : ⭐⭐⭐
- **In 71st Place:**
- Jennifer Shackford
- **In 72nd Place:**
- Angela Bixby
- **In 73rd Place:**
- Nadia Shapiro
- **In 74th Place:**
- Joyce Markwick
- **In 75th Place:**
- Robert Rodriguez

TOP 80 MEDIUMS IN THE WORLD : ⭐⭐⭐
- **In 79th Place:**
- Cassandra Larsen
- **In 80th Place:**
- Deidre Madsen

TOP 85 MEDIUMS IN THE WORLD : ⭐⭐⭐
- **In 81st Place:**
- Jill Beiler
- **In 82nd Place:**
- Matthew Brandau
- **In 83rd Place:**
- Carrie-Anne Hartley Silkowski
- **In 85th Place:**
- Angela Kruszka

TOP 90 MEDIUMS IN THE WORLD : ⭐⭐⭐
- **In 86th Place:**
- Charlene Hicks
- **In 87th Place:**
- Rachel Marie
- **In 88th Place:**
- Jeannine Bakriges
- **In 89th Place:**
- Sandra Nemet
- **In 90th Place:**
- Diane Williams

TOP 95 MEDIUMS IN THE WORLD : ⭐⭐⭐
- **In 92nd Place:**
- Lisa Bousson
- **In 95th Place:**
- Agnes Obrzanowska

TOP 100 MEDIUMS IN THE WORLD : ⭐⭐⭐
- **In 96th Place:**
- Aurora Rose aka Stephanie Stinnett
- **In 97th Place:**
- Catherine Dougherty
- **In 98th Place:**
- DC Love
- **In 100th Place:**
- Joshua John

TOP 105 MEDIUMS IN THE WORLD : ⭐⭐⭐
- **In 101st Place:**
- Kristen Leona
- **In 104th Place:**
- Shereece Davison
- **In 105th Place:**

- Simone Key (UK/USA)

TOP 110 MEDIUMS IN THE WORLD : ⭐⭐⭐
- **In 109th Place:**
- Adam Bernstein
- **In 110th Place:**
- Bella Mason

TOP 115 MEDIUMS IN THE WORLD : ⭐⭐⭐
- **In 111th Place:**
- Catherine Birkhimer
- **In 112th Place:**
- Dianne Winbauer
- **In 113th Place:**
- Donna McGrath

TOP 120 MEDIUMS IN THE WORLD : ⭐⭐⭐
- **In 116th Place:**
- Jen Queen (USA)
- **In117th Place:**
- Joshua John (USA)
- **In 118th Place:**
- Kelly Mackey (Ireland/Irlande)
- **In 119th Place:**
- Linda Jolley (USA)
- **In 120th Place:**
- Medium Irene (USA)

TOP 125 MEDIUMS IN THE WORLD : Les 125 meilleurs Médiums du monde. ⭐⭐⭐
- **In 121st Place:**
- Medium Sherie (Canada)
- **In 122nd Place:**
- Nodira Standard (USA)

- **In 123rd Place:**
- Noemia Walaska (USA)
- **In 124th Place:**
- Rachel S. Kohler (USA)
- **In 125th Place:**
- Regina Norlinde (USA)

TOP 130 MEDIUMS IN THE WORLD : Les 130 meilleurs Médiums du monde. ⭐⭐⭐

- **In 126th Place:**
- Rosine Bramly (France)
- **In 127th Place:**
- Samantha McGovern (USA)
- **In 128th Place:**
- Saundra Greene (USA)
- **In 129th Place:**
- Thomas John (USA)
- **In 130th Place:**
- Tina Carey (USA)

TOP 135 MEDIUMS IN THE WORLD : Les 135 meilleurs Médiums du monde. ⭐⭐⭐

- **In 131st Place:**
- Ursula Kalin (USA)
- **In 132nd Place:**
- Alex Treglazoff (USA)
- **In 133rdPlace:**
- Anthony Morgann (USA)
- **In 134th Place:**
- Astrid Stromberg (USA)
- **In 135th Place:**
- Barbara Almond (USA)

TOP 140 MEDIUMS IN THE WORLD : Les 135 meilleurs Médiums du monde. ⭐⭐⭐

- **In 136th Place:**
- Barbara DeLong (USA)
- **In 137th Place:**
- Belinda Bentley (USA)
- **In 138th Place:**
- Bonnie Albers (USA)
- **In 139th Place:**
- Bree Peltier (USA)
- **In 140th Place:**
- Cathie Bradshaw (USA)

TOP 145 MEDIUMS IN THE WORLD : Les 135 meilleurs Médiums du monde.
- **In 141st Place:**
- Christina Nelson (USA)
- **In 142nd Place:**
- Cindy Greene (USA)
- **In 143rd Place:**
- Claire Braddock (USA).
- **In 144th Place:**
- Dawn Bothie (USA)
- **In 145th Place:**
- Dawn Mystic Haven (USA)

TOP 150 MEDIUMS IN THE WORLD : Les 135 meilleurs Médiums du monde. ⭐⭐⭐
- **In 146th Place:**
- DC Love (USA)
- **In 147th Place:**
- Deborah Adams Livingston (UK/Angleterre)
- **In 148th Place:**
- Debra Leblanc (USA)
- **In 149th Place:**
- Dianne Benier (Australia/Australie)
- **In 150th Place:**
- Eileen Boettcher (USA)

TOP 155 MEDIUMS IN THE WORLD : Les 135 meilleurs Médiums du monde. ⭐⭐⭐

- **In 151st Place:**
- Elisjah Anderzen (USA)
- **In 152nd Place:**
- Eric Glyn (USA)
- **In 153rd Place:**
- Eric van Riessen (Netherlands/Pays Bas)
- **In 154th Place:**
- Feebee McIntyre (USA)
- **In 155th Place:**
- Gemini Rose (USA)

TOP 160 MEDIUMS IN THE WORLD : Les 135 meilleurs Médiums du monde. ⭐⭐⭐

- **In 156th Place:**
- Georgia Marantos (USA)
- **In 156th Place:**
- Greg Kehn (USA)
- **In 158th Place:**
- Helen DaVita (UK/Angleterre)
- **In 159th Place:**
- Hillary Freitas (USA)
- **In 160th Place:**
- Hoyt Robinette (USA)

TOP 165 MEDIUMS IN THE WORLD : Les 135 meilleurs Médiums du monde. ⭐⭐⭐

- **In 161st Place:**
- Irene Hope Burke (USA)
- **In 162nd Place:**
- Jean Koly (Luxembourg)
- **In 163rd Place:**
- Jeanne Clock (USA)
- **In 164th Place:**
- Jonna Kay Carlson (USA)

- **In 165th Place:**
- Joy Brisbane (Australia/Australie)

TOP 170 MEDIUMS IN THE WORLD : Les 135 meilleurs Médiums du monde. ⭐⭐⭐
- **In 166th Place:**
- Karen Cote (USA)
- **In 167th Place:**
- Karleen Heller (USA)
- **In 168th Place:**
- Kimberley Smith (USA)
- **In 169th Place:**
- Lynn Bleasdale (USA)
- **In 170th Place:**
- Mama Aisha (Lebanon/Liban)

TOP 175 MEDIUMS IN THE WORLD : Les 135 meilleurs Médiums du monde. ⭐⭐⭐
- **In 171st Place:**
- Abu Khaled (UAE)
- **In 172nd Place:**
- Mandy Thompson (USA)
- **In 173rd Place:**
- Marisa Ryan (USA)
- **In 174th Place:**
- Martin F. Jones (UK/Angleterre)
- **In 175th Place:**
- Matthew Smith (USA)

TOP 180 MEDIUMS IN THE WORLD : Les 135 meilleurs Médiums du monde. ⭐⭐⭐
- **In 176th Place:**
- Maureen Murnan (UK/Angleterre)
- **In 177th Place:**
- Oktobre Taylor (USA)

65

- **In 178ᵗʰ Place:**
- Patricia O'Boyle, Reverend (USA)
- **In 179ᵗʰ Place:**
- Patrick De Haan (USA)
- **In 180ᵗʰ Place:**
- Phill Renton (UK/Angleterre)

TOP 185 MEDIUMS IN THE WORLD : Les 135 meilleurs Médiums du monde. ⭐⭐⭐

- **In 181st Place:**
- Renee Richards (USA)
- **In 182nd Place:**
- Richard Schoeller (USA)
- **In 183rd Place:**
- Ryan Smith (USA)
- **In 184ᵗʰ Place:**
- Sammie Jo Huffstetler (USA)
- **In 185ᵗʰ Place:**
- Sarah McCoy (USA)

TOP 190 MEDIUMS IN THE WORLD : Les 135 meilleurs Médiums du monde. ⭐⭐⭐

- **In 186ᵗʰ Place:**
- Sarina St. John (USA)
- **In 187ᵗʰ Place:**
- Shanon Corkins (USA)
- **In 188ᵗʰ Place:**
- Sharon Harding (Australia/Australie)
- **In 189ᵗʰ Place:**
- Sondra Sneed (USA)
- **In 190ᵗʰ Place:**
- Stevie Pierce (USA)

TOP 195 MEDIUMS IN THE WORLD : Les 135 meilleurs Médiums du monde. ⭐⭐⭐

- **In 191st Place:**
- Susan Sanderford (USA)

- **In 192nd Place:**
- Susie Grimett (USA)
- **In 193rd Place:**
- Terri Daniel (USA)
- **In 194th Place:**
- Timitha Bryan (USA)
- **In 195th Place:**
- Trish Woods (USA)

TOP 200 MEDIUMS IN THE WORLD : Les 135 meilleurs Médiums du monde. ⭐⭐⭐
- **In 196th Place:**
- Venus Andrecht (USA)
- **In 197th Place:**
- Wendy Reinli (USA)
- **In 198th Place:**
- Helena Vestin (Sweden/Suede)

NOTE: Names of lightworkers who have received less than 3 votes were deleted. (Approximately 713 names)

*** *** ***

Last Year's Best Mediums in the World.

TOP 5 IN THE WORLD: 5 STARS RATING

- #1: 2365 votes. Patti Negri (USA). Last year's rank: Number 1 in the world and Number 1 in the United States.
- #1: 2365 votes. Michelle Whitedove (USA). Last year's rank: Number 17 in the world and Number 10 in the United States.

- #2: 1989 votes. Jennifer Wallens. (USA).
- #3: 1765 votes. Kimberly Ward (USA).
- #4: 1431 votes. Suzanne Grace (USA). Last year's rank: Number 60 in the world.
- #4: 1431 votes. Michelle Whitedove (USA). Last year's rank: Number 17 in the world and Number 10 in the United States.

TOP 10 IN THE WORLD: 5 STARS RATING

- #7: 601 votes. Shannon Leischner (USA). Last year's rank: Number 60 in the world.
- #8: 313 votes. Kim Russo (USA).
- #9: 244 votes. Lorie Johnson (USA).
- #10: 231 votes. Linda Salvin, Ph.D. (USA).

TOP 15 IN THE WORLD: 4 STARS RATING

- #11: 161 votes. Van Doren Figueredo (USA).
- #12: 160 votes. Keli Michaels (USA).
- #12: 160 votes. Karina Voroshilova (USA).
- #13: 159 votes. Sherrie Hurd-Roufosse (USA).
- #15: 109 votes. Amelia Pisano Scozzari (USA/Canada).

TOP 20 IN THE WORLD: 4 STARS RATING

- #16: 100 votes. Cassandra Larsen. (USA).
- #17: 71 votes. Matthew Brandau (USA).
- #18: 70 votes. Sandra Nemet (USA).
- #19: 47 votes. Charlene Hicks (USA).
- #20: 39 votes. Carrie-Anne Hartley Silkowski (USA).

TOP 25 IN THE WORLD: 2 STARS RATING

- #21: 37 votes. Simone Key (USA).
- #23: 32 votes. Aurora Rose aka Stephanie Stinnett (USA).
- #24: 30 votes. Jennifer Shackford (USA).

- #25: 29 votes. Tina Saelee (USA/Thailand). Last year's rank: Number 50 in the world.
- #25: 29 votes. Catherine Dougherty (USA).

TOP 30 IN THE WORLD: 1 STAR RATING

- #27: 28 votes. Agnes Obrzanowska (USA).
- #28: 27 votes. Regina Norlinde (USA).
- #29: 26 votes. Donna McGrath (USA).
- #30: 12 votes. Bella Mason (USA).
- #30: 12 votes. Kimberley Smith (USA).
- #30: 12 votes. Kimberley Smith (USA).

TOP 35 IN THE WORLD: 1 STAR RATING

- #31: 11 votes. Rachel S. Kohler (USA).
- #32: 10 votes. Alex Treglazoff (USA).
- #32: 10 votes. Adam Bernstein (USA).
- #33: 9 votes. Dianne Winbauer (USA).
- #33: 9 votes. Catherine Birkhimer (USA).
- #34: 8 votes. Samantha McGovern (USA).
- #34: 8 votes. Noemia Walaska (USA).
- #34: 7 votes. Nodira Standard (USA).

TOP 40 IN THE WORLD: 1 STAR RATING

- #35: 6 votes. Hoyt Robinette (USA).
- #35: 6 votes. Doyle Ward (USA).
- #35: 6 votes. Wendy Reinli (USA).
- #37: 4 votes. Sarina St. John (USA).
- #38: 3 votes. Belinda Bentley (USA).
- #38: 3 votes. Matthew Smith (USA).
- #39: 2 votes. Jonna Kay Carlson (USA).

OTHERS

- 1 vote. Alex Treglazoff (USA).

- 1 vote. Anthony Morgann (USA).
- 1 vote. Claire Braddock (USA).
- 1 vote. Gemini Rose (USA).
- 1 vote. Hillary Freitas (USA).
- 1 vote. Jamie Butler (USA).
- 1 vote. Joshua John (USA).
- 1 vote. Linda Jolley (USA).
- 1 vote. Medium Irene (USA).
- 1 vote. Medium Sherie (Canada/USA).
- 1 vote. Saundra Greene (USA).
- 1 vote. Thomas John (USA).
- 1 vote. Ursula Kalin (USA).
- 1 vote. Isabelle Dawes (USA).

*** *** ***

THE BEST MEDIUMS IN THE UNITED STATES

Top 5 mediums in the United States in this rank order: ★★★★★

#1. Patti Negri
#2. Jennifer Wallens
#3. Tracy Lee Nash
#4. Vickie Gay
#5. Suzanne Grace

From left to right: 1-Patti Negri. 2-Jennifer Wallens.

Tracy Lee Nash. 3-Vickie Gay.

Suzanne Grace

TOP 10 MEDIUMS IN THE UNITED STATES IN THIS RANK ORDER: ★★★★★

#6. John Cappello
#7. Rita Berkowitz
#8. Jessicca Cannon Haas
#9. Lorraine Roe
#10. Melissa Berman

John Cappello. Rita Berkowitz.

Jessicca Cannon Haas. Lorraine Roe

Melissa Berman.

TOP 15 MEDIUMS IN THE UNITED STATES IN THIS RANK ORDER: ★★★★★

#11. Ruth Larkin
#12. Lisa Williams
#13. Vicki Monroe
#14. Rick Hayes
#15. Cathy Towle

Ruth Larkin. Lisa Williams.

Vicki Monroe. Rick Hayes

Cathy Towle.

**TOP 20 MEDIUMS IN THE UNITED STATES IN THIS
RANK ORDER:** ★★★★★
#16. B. Anne Gehman, Reverend
#17. Daved Beck
#18. Magdalena Gjesvold
#19. Tiffany Powers
#20. Katherine Glass
#20. Sherie Hurd Roufosse.

Reverend B. Anne Gehman. Daved Beck.

Magdalena Gjesvold. Tiffany Powers.

Katherine Glass. Sherie Hurd Roufosse

TOP 25 MEDIUMS IN THE UNITED STATES IN THIS RANK ORDER: ★★★★★

#21. Dena Flanagan
#22. Jake Samoyedny
#23. Jennifer Shackford
#24. Karina Voroshilova
#25. Belle Salisbury

Dena Flanagan. Jake Samoyedny.

Jennifer Shackford. Karina Voroshilova.

Belle Salisbiry

TOP 30 MEDIUMS IN THE UNITED STATES IN THIS RANK ORDER: ★★★★
#26. Nadia Shapiro
#27. Cassandra Larsen
#28. Deidre Madsen
#29. Jill Beiler
#30. Carrie-Anne Hartley Silkowski

Nadia Shapiro. Cassandra Larsen

Deidre Madsen. Carrie-Anne Hartley Silkowski.

TOP 30 MEDIUMS IN THE UNITED STATES IN THIS RANK ORDER: ☆☆☆☆

#31. Matthew Brandau
#32. Charlene Hicks
#33. Rachel Marie
#34. Jeannine Bakriges
#35. Sandra Nemet
#35. Deborah Leblanc (USA)

NOTE: Names of lightworkers who have received less than 3 votes were deleted.

*** *** ***

Last Year's Best Mediums in the United States: Listing by Rank and Number of Votes.

TOP 5 IN THE UNITED STATES: 5 STARS RATING

- #1: 2365 votes. Patti Negri. Last year's rank: Number 1 in the world and Number 1 in the United States.
- #1: 2365 votes. Michelle Whitedove. Last year's rank: Number 17 in the world and Number 10 in the United States.
- #2: 1989 votes. Jennifer Wallens.
- #3: 1765 votes. Kimberly Ward.
- #4: 1431 votes. Suzanne Grace. Last year's rank: Number 60 in the world.
- #5: 601 votes. Shannon Leischner. Last year's rank: Number 60 in the world.

TOP 10 IN THE UNITED STATES: 5 STARS RATING

- #6: 313 votes. Kim Russo.
- #7: 245 votes. Lorie Johnson.
- #8: 231 votes. Linda Salvin, Ph.D.
- #9: 161 votes. Van Doren Figueredo.
- #10: 160 votes. Keli Michaels.
- #10: 160 votes. Karina Voroshilova.

TOP 15 IN THE UNITED STATES: 4 STARS RATING

- #11: 159 votes. Sherrie Hurd-Roufosse.
- #12: 109 votes. Amelia Pisano Scozzari (Canada/USA).
- #13: 100 votes. Cassandra Larsen.
- #14: 70 votes. Sandra Nemet.
- #15: 71 votes. Matthew Smith.

- #15: 71 votes. Matthew Brandau.

TOP 20 IN THE UNITED STATES: 3 STARS RATING

- #16:48 votes. Donna McGrath.
- #17: 47 votes. Charlene Hicks.
- #18: 39 votes. Carrie-Anne Hartley Silkowski.
- #19: 37 votes. Simone Key.
- #20: 32 votes. Aurora Rose aka Stephanie Stinnett.

TOP 25 IN THE UNITED STATES: 2 STARS RATING

- #21: 30 votes. Jennifer Shackford.
- #22: 29 votes. Catherine Dougherty.
- #23: 28 votes. Agnes Obrzanowska.
- #24: 27 votes. Regina Norlinde.
- #25: 12 votes. Bella Mason.

TOP 30 IN THE UNITED STATES: 1 STAR RATING

- #26: 12 votes. Kimberley Smith.
- #26: 11 votes. Rachel S. Kohler
- #27: 10 votes. Alex Treglazoff.
- #27: 10 votes. Adam Bernstein.
- #28: 9 votes. Dianne Winbauer.
- #28: 9 votes. Catherine Birkhimer
- #29: 8 votes. Samantha McGovern.
- #29: 8 votes. Noemia Walaska.
- #30: 6 votes. Hoyt Robinette.
- #30: 6 votes. Doyle Ward.
- #30: 6 votes. Wendy Reinli.

TOP 35 IN THE UNITED STATES:

- #31: 4 votes. Sarina St. John.
- #32: 3 votes. Belinda Bentley.
- #32: 3 votes. Belinda Bentley.
- #33: 2 votes. Jonna Kay Carlson.

OTHERS

- 1 vote. Anthony Morgann.
- 1 vote. Arice Miranda.
- 1 vote. Claire Braddock.
- 1 vote. Gemini Rose.
- 1 vote. Hillary Freitas.
- 1 vote. Jamie Butler.
- 1 vote. Linda Jolley.
- 1 vote. Saundra Greene.
- 1 vote. Thomas John.
- 1 vote. Ursula Kalin.
- 1 vote. Joshua John.
- 1 vote. Isabelle Dawes.

*** *** ***

BEST PHYSICAL MEDIUM IN THE US

- **In 10th Place:**
- Mychael Shane, Rev. (USA)

Reverend Mychael Shane.

*** *** ***

AMERICANS WHO MADE THE LIST OF THE BEST PSYCHICS IN THE WORLD.

In alphabetical order.

A

- Abby Rose Newman (USA)
- Allison Dubois (USA)
- Allison Hayes (USA)
- Amanda Hufford (USA)
- Amelia Armstrong (USA)
- Amy Cavanaugh (USA)
- Andrew Anderson (USA)
- Andrew Brewer (USA)
- Angela Bixby (USA)
- Angela Kruszka (USA)
- Angela Lusk (USA)
- Angie Mitchell (USA)
- Anna Galliers (UK/Angleterre)

- Anna Robles Simon (USA)
- Anthony Morgan (USA)
- April Ashbrook (USA)
- Arice Miranda (USA)
- Arice Miranda (USA)
- Ashlei Yatron (USA)
- Ashley Riley (USA)
- Astrid (USA)

B

- Barbara Delong (USA)
- Barbara Mackey (USA)
- Bee Herz (USA)
- Bella Mason (USA)
- Belle Salisbury (USA)
- Betsy Cohen (USA)
- Bonnie Albers (USA)
- Brandy Marie Miller (USA)
- Bree Peltier (USA)
- Brenda Tenerelli (USA)

C

- Candy Odonnell (USA)
- Cari Roy (USA)
- Carla Baron (USA)
- Carmen Harra, PhD (USA)
- Carole Lynne (USA)
- Carolyn Myss (USA)
- Cassandra Larsen (USA)
- Catherine Roller (USA)
- Celia Caulfield (USA)
- Chanda Reaves (USA)
- Char Margolis (USA)
- Chip Coffey (USA)
- Chris Avery Cole (USA)
- Chris White (USA)
- Christina Nelson (USA)
- Christine Corda (USA)

- Cindy Greene (USA)
- Claire Braddock (USA)
- Claire Candy Hough (USA)
- Claudia Johnson (USA)
- Colette Baron-Reid (USA)
- Concetta Bertoldi (USA)
- Corbie Mitleid (USA)
- Corrine DeWinter (USA)
- Coryelle Kramer (USA)

D

- Danielle Mackinnon (USA)
- Darren Green (USA)
- Daved Beck (USA)
- Dawn Bothie (USA)
- Dawn Hiruko (USA)
- Dawn Mystic Haven (USA)
- Dawn Short (USA)
- DC Love (USA)
- Delia Yeager (USA)
- Dena Flanagan (USA)
- Derek Calibre (USA)
- Destiny (USA)
- Diana Richardson (USA)
- Diane Hamilton (USA)
- Diane Hiller (USA)
- Diane Williams (USA)
- Dolores Cardelucci (USA)
- Doreen Virtue (USA)
- Dorothy Allyson (USA)
- Dorothy Morgan (USA)
- Doyle Ward (USA)

E

- Echo Bodine (USA)
- Eileen Boettcher (USA)
- Elisjah Anderzen (USA)
- Elizabeth Baron (USA)

- Elizabeth Joyce (USA)
- Elizabeth Wissbaum (USA)
- Eric Glyn (USA)

F

- Feebee McIntyre (USA)
- Frank Andrews (USA)

G

- Gary Wimmer (USA)
- Gayle Kirk (USA)
- Gemini Rose (USA)
- Georgia Cuningham (USA)
- Gerta Lestock (USA)
- Greta Alexander (USA)

H

- Harriette Knight (USA)
- Heather Coleman-Ibrahim (USA)
- Helene Frisch (USA)

I

- Isabelle Dawes (USA)

J

- Jake Samoyedny (USA)
- James Demos (USA)
- James Van Praagh (USA)
- Jamie Butler (USA)
- Jamie Clark (USA)
- Jamie DiMarco (USA)

- Jan Drake Bakke (USA)
- Jane Borowski (USA)
- Janine Regan Sinclair (USA)
- Jean Salch (USA)
- Jeanne Clock (USA)
- Jeannine G Wand (USA)
- Jennifer Shackford (USA)
- Jennifer Wallens (USA)
- Jeremie Leischner (USA)
- Jessica Costello (USA)
- Jessicca Cannon Haas (USA)
- Jethro Smith (USA)
- Jill Dahne (USA)
- Joan Bunyan (USA)
- Joanne Gerber (USA)
- John Cappello (USA)
- John Edward (USA)
- John Harricharan (USA)
- John Holland (USA)
- Jonna Kay Carlson (USA)
- Joshua John (USA)
- Joyce Keller (USA)
- Judy Hevenly (USA)

K

- Karen Page (USA)
- Karleen Heller (USA)
- Kate Sitka (USA)
- Kathlyn Rhea (USA)
- Kay Jacobs (USA)
- Keli Michaels (USA)
- Kelli Faulkner (USA)
- Kelly Coulter (USA)
- Ken Morris (USA)
- Kenneth Bentley (USA)
- Kim Russo (USA)
- Kimberly Ward (USA)
- Kristen Lavespere (USA)
- Krzysztof "Kris" Chmielewski (USA)

- Kyamrian Samedov (Azerbaijan)

L

- Laura Alden Kamm (USA)
- Laura Jackson (USA)
- Laura Mendelsohn (USA)
- Lee Papa (USA)
- Legina Waters Smith (USA)
- Leslie Hinojosa (USA)
- Linda Irwin (USA)
- Linda Jolley Richards (USA)
- Linda Lauren (USA)
- Linda Salvin, Ph.D. (USA)
- Lisa Williams (USA)
- Litany Burns (USA)
- Lori Green-Connell (USA)
- Lori Karras (USA)
- Lorie Johnson (USA)
- Lorraine Lush (USA)
- Lorraine Roe (USA)
- Love Grado (USA)
- Lydia Clar (USA)
- Lydia DiVincenzo (USA)
- Lynn Bleasdale (USA)
- Lynn Van-Praagh-Gratton (USA)

M

- Marcy Currier (USA)
- Marla Phillips (USA)
- Mary Ennis (USA)
- Mary T. Browne (USA)
- Matina (USA)
- Matt Fraser (USA)
- Matthew Brandau (USA)
- Maya Britan (USA)
- Melissa Berman (USA)
- Melissa Stamps (USA)

- Michelle Gilhouse (USA)
- Michelle Whitedove (USA)
- Micki Dahne (USA)
- Mike Loop (USA)
- Misty Sevy (USA)

N

- Nancy Bradley (USA)
- Nancy Feranec (USA)
- Nancy Marlowe (USA)
- Nancy Myer (USA)
- Nicki Bonfilio (USA)
- Noelle Garneau (USA)
- Noreen Renier (USA)

P

- Paddy Chaver (USA)
- Pam Coronado (USA)
- Pamela Cummins (USA)
- Pamela Cushman (USA)
- Patricia Masters (USA)
- Patricia Mischell (USA)
- Patrick De Haan (USA)
- Patti Negri (USA)
- Peg Jones (USA)
- PennyC (USA)
- Peter Chef (USA)
- Peter J. Serraino (USA)
- Phil Jordan (USA)

Q

- Quinton Carlson (USA)

R

- Rachel Marie (USA)

- Rachel Norway (USA)
- Rick Waid (USA)
- Robert Bourassa (USA)
- Robert F. Burke (USA)
- Robert Rodriguez (USA)
- Robyn Fritz (USA)
- Rochelle Sparrow (USA)
- Roger Nobles (USA)
- Rosalee Karls (USA)
- Rosemary Altea (USA)
- Roxanne Elizabeth Useman (USA)
- Roy Worley (USA)
- Ryan Smith (USA)

S

- Sally Brustowicz (USA)
- Sandra Greene (USA)
- Sandra Nemet (USA)
- Sarah LaBrie (USA)
- Sarah McCoy (USA)
- Sarah Meredith (USA)
- Shannon Leischner (USA)
- Shanon Corkins (USA)
- Sharon Kissane (USA)
- Sharon Pugh (USA)
- Sheena Metal (USA)
- Sherie Hurd Roufusse (USA)
- Smirti Mukherjee (USA)
- Solana (USA)
- Sondra Sneed (USA)
- Sprinkles Nixon (USA)
- Stacey Wolf-James (USA)
- Stan Kestrel (USA)
- Stephen Robinson (USA)
- Sue Dalimonte (USA)
- Sue Raye (USA)
- Sunhee and Chinhee Park (USA)
- Susan Rowlen (USA)
- Susan Sanderford (USA)
- Suzanne Grace (USA)

T

- Tarah Harper (USA)
- Terri James (USA)
- Terry and Linda Jamison (USA)
- Theresa Caputo (USA)
- Thomas John (USA)
- Timitha Bryan (USA)
- Tori Allah (USA)
- Tracy Lee Nash (USA)

U

- Ula Yule (USA)
- Ursula Kalin (USA)

V

- Venus Andrecht (USA)
- Vianne Higgins (USA)
- Vicki L. Robinson (USA)
- Vickie Gay (USA)

*** *** ***

AMERICANS WHO MADE THE LIST OF THE WORLD'S BEST PSYCHICS.
(Out of approximately 850,000 psychics in 83 countries)
THE GREATEST PSYCHICS IN MODERN TIME

In national rank order.

TOP 5: ★★★★★
- ☐ **In 1st Place:**
- ☐ Patti Negri (USA)
- ☐ **In 2nd Place:**
- ☐ Jennifer Wallens (USA)

- [ ] **In 3rd Place:**
- [ ] Tracy Lee Nash (USA)
- [ ] Michelle Whitedove (USA)
- [ ] **In 4th Place:**
- [ ] Sunhee and Chinhee Park (USA)

Patti Negri. 2-Jennifer Wallens. 3-Tracy Lee Nash.

Michelle Whitedove. Sunhee Park and Chinhee Park (USA).

TOP 10: ★★★★★
- [ ] **In 8th Place:**
- [ ] John Holland (USA)
- [ ] **In 9th Place:**
- [ ] Micki Dahne (USA)
- [ ] **In 10th Place:**
- [ ] Concetta Bertoldi (USA)

☐   Allison Hayes (USA)

John Holland.

Micki Dahne. Concetta Bertoldi.

TOP 15: ★★★★★
- **In 12th Place:**
- Suzanne Grace (USA)

Suzanne Grace.

TOP 20: ★★★★★

- **In 16th Place:**
- Vickie Gay (USA)
- **In 17th Place:**
- Dianne Hiller (USA)
- **In 18th Place**
- Jessicca Cannon Haas (USA)
- PennyC (USA)
- **In 19th Place:**
- Sherie Hurd Roufusse (USA)
- Melissa Stamps (USA)
- **In 20th Place**
- Lorraine Roe (USA)

Vickie Gay

Dianne Hiller. Jessicca Cannon Haas.

PennyC. Sherie Hurd Roufusse.

Melissa Stamps. Lorraine Roe.

TOP 25: ★★★★★
- **In 21st Place:**
- Joyce Keller (USA)
- Dena Flanagan (USA)
- **In 22nd Place:**
- John Cappello (USA)
- **In 23rd Place:**
- Jethro Smith (USA)
- **In 24th Place:**
- Kimberly Ward (USA)
- **In 25th Place:**
- Corbie Mitleid (USA)
- Doyle Ward. (USA)

Joyce Keller. Dena Flanagan.

John Cappello (USA).

Jethro Smith. Kimberly Ward.

Corbie Mitleid. Doyle Ward.

TOP 30: ★★★★★

- **In 26th Place:**
- Irene Hope Burke (USA)
- Shannon Leischner (USA)
- **In 27th Place:**
- Roxanne Elizabeth Usleman (USA)
- Angela Bixby (USA)
- **In 28th Place:**
- Frank Andrews (USA)
- **In 29th Place:**
- Kim Russo (USA)
- **In 30th Place:**
- John Harricharan (USA)
- April Ashbrook (USA)

Irene Hope Burke. Shannon Leischner.

Roxanne Elizabeth Usleman. Angela Bixby.

Frank Andrews. Kim Ruso.

TOP 35: ★★★★★

- **In 31st Place:**
- John Harricharan (USA)
- **In 32nd Place:**
- Stacey Wolf-James (USA)

- Bella Mason (USA)
- **In 33rd Place:**
- Carmen Harra, PhD (USA)
- **In 34th Place:**
- Elizabeth Joyce (USA)

TOP 40: ★★★★★
- **In 36th Place:**
- Greta Alexander (USA)
- **In 37th Place:**
- Laura Mendelsohn (USA)
- **In 39th Place:**
- Linda Lauren (USA)
- **In 40th Place:**
- Karen Page (USA)

TOP 45: ★★★★★
- **In 41st Place:**
- Jake Samoyedny (USA)
- **In 42nd Place:**
- Krzysztof "Kris" Chmielewski (USA)
- **In 43rd Place:**
- Robert Rodriguez (USA)
- **In 44th Place:**
- Allison Dubois (USA)
- **In 45th Place:**
- James Van Praagh (USA)

TOP 50: ★★★★★
- **In 47th Place:**
- Litany Burns (USA)
- **In 50th Place:**
- Mary T. Browne (USA)

TOP 55: ★★★★★
- **In 51st Place:**
- Patricia Mischell (USA)
- **In 52nd Place:**
- Daved Beck (USA)
- **In 53rd Place:**
- Lorie Johnson (USA)
- **In 55th Place:**
- Doreen Virtue (USA)

TOP 60: ★★★★★
- **In 56th Place:**
- Doreen Virtue (USA)
- **In 57th Place:**
- Doreen Virtue (USA)
- **In 58th Place:**
- Kathlyn Rhea. (USA)

TOP 65: ★★★★★
- **In 65th Place:**
- Noelle Garneau (USA)

TOP 70: ★★★★★
- **In 67th Place:**
- Char Margolis (USA)
- **In 69th Place:**
- Lisa Williams (USA)
- **In 70th Place:**
- Mary Ennis (USA)

TOP 75: ★★★★
- **In 72nd Place:**
- Rosemary Altea (USA)
- **In 74th Place:**
- Carla Baron (USA)

- In 75th **Place:**
- Chip Coffey (USA)

TOP 80: ★★★★
- **In 78th Place:**
- Patricia Masters (USA)
- **In 80th Place:**
- Stephen Robinson (USA)

TOP 85: ★★★★
- **In 82nd Place:**
- Janine Regan Sinclair (USA)
- **In 85th Place:**
- Lorraine Lush (USA)

TOP 90: ★★★★
- **In 86th Place**
- Joanne Gerber (USA)

TOP 95: ★★★★
- **In 92nd Place**
- Lori Karras (USA)
- **In 93rd Place**
- Colette Baron-Reid (USA)
- **In 94th Place:**
- Tarah Harper (USA)

TOP 100: ★★★★
- **In 96th Place:**
- Claudia Johnson (USA)

TOP 105: ★★★★

- **In 101st Place:**
- Keli Michaels (USA)
- **In 102nd Place:**
- Barbara Mackey (USA)
- **In 105th Place**
- Joan Bunyan (USA)

TOP 110: ★★★★

- **In 106th Place:**
- Lydia Clar (USA)
- **In 109th Place:**

TOP 115: ★★★★

- **In 111th Place:**
- Keli Michaels (USA)
- **In 112th Place:**
- John Edward (USA)
- **In 114th Place:**
- Noreen Renier (USA)

TOP 120: ★★★★

- **In 116th Place:**
- Jamie Butler (USA)

TOP 125: ★★★★

- **In 121st Place:**
- Nancy Myer (USA)
- **In 122nd Place:**
- Tarah Harper (USA)
- **In 123rd Place:**
- Linda Salvin, Ph.D. (USA)

TOP 130: ★★★★

- **In 128th Place:**

- Andrew Brewer (USA)
- **In 130th Place:**
- Sandra Nemet (USA)

TOP 135: ★★★★
- **In 131st Place:**
- Judy Hevenly (USA)
- **In 132nd Place:**
- Helene Frisch (USA)
- **In 133rd Place:**
- Terry and Linda Jamison (USA)
- **In 135th Place:**
- Abby Rose Newman (USA)

TOP 140: ★★★★
- **In 137th Place:**
- Jan Drake Bakke (USA)
- **In 138th Place:**
- Maya Britan (USA)
- **In 140th Place:**
- Dorothy Allyson (USA)

TOP 145: ★★★★
- **In 142nd Place:**
- Adrienne Miles (USA)
- **In 143rd Place:**
- Bee Herz (USA)

TOP 150: ★★★★
- **In 147th Place:**
- Pam Coronado (USA)
- **In 148th Place:**
- Thomas John (USA)
- **In 149th Place:**
- Chris Avery Cole (USA)

TOP 155: ⭐⭐⭐⭐
- **In 151st Place:**
- Theresa Caputo (USA)
- **In 153rd Place:**
- Marla Phillips (USA)
- **In 154th Place:**
- Karina Voroshilova (USA)

TOP 160: ⭐⭐⭐⭐
- **In 156th Place:**
- Sue Raye (USA)
- **In 157th Place:**
- Amelia Pisano Scozzari (Canada/USA)
- **In 158th Place:**
- Jennifer Shackford (USA)
- **In 159th Place:**
- Belle Salisbury (USA)
- **In 160th Place:**
- Dawn Short (USA)

TOP 165: ⭐⭐⭐⭐
- **In 161st Place:**
- Nicki Bonfilio (USA)
- **In 162nd Place:**
- Sharon Pugh (USA)
- **In 164th Place:**
- Gary Wimmer (USA)

TOP 170: ⭐⭐⭐⭐
- **In 167th Place:**
- Peg Jones (USA)
- **In 168th Place:**
- Rachel Marie (USA)
- **In 170th Place:**
- Sally Brustowicz (USA)

TOP 175: ★★★★
- In 171st Place:
- Amelia Armstrong (USA)
- In 172nd Place:
- Ashlei Yatron (USA)
- In 173rd Place:
- Ashlei Yatron (USA)
- In 174th Place:
- Betsy Cohen (USA)
- In 175th Place:
- Cassandra Larsen (USA)

TOP 180: ★★★★
- In 177th Place:
- Elizabeth Baron (USA)
- In 178th Place:
- Jamie Clark (USA)
- In 180th Place:
- Kelly Coulter (USA)

TOP 185: ★★★
- In 181st Place:
- Laura Jackson (USA)
- In 182nd Place:
- Linda Irwin (USA)
- In 184th Place:
- Lynn Bleasdale (USA)
- In 185th Place:
- Nancy Bradley (USA)

TOP 190: ★★★
- In 186th Place:
- Pamela Cushman (USA)
- In 187th Place:
- Vicki L. Robinson (USA)

- **In 188th Place:**
- Amanda Hufford (USA)
- **In 190th Place:**
- Angela Lusk (USA)

TOP 195: ⭐⭐⭐
- **In 191st Place:**
- Ashley Riley (USA)
- **In 192nd Place:**
- Astrid (USA)
- **In 193rd Place:**
- Coryelle Kramer (USA)
- **In 194th Place:**
- Dawn Hiruko (USA)
- **In 195th Place:**
- Diane Williams (USA)

TOP 200: ⭐⭐⭐
- **In 196th Place:**
- Gayle Kirk (USA)
- **In 197th Place:**
- Georgia Cuningham (USA)
- **In 198th Place:**
- Harriette Knight (USA)
- **In 199th Place:**
- Jane Borowski (USA)
- **In 200nd Place:**
- Jessica Costello (USA)

TOP 205: ⭐⭐⭐
- **In 201st Place:**
- Linda Jolley Richards (USA)
- **In 203rd Place:**
- Mariah Crawford (USA)
- **In 205th Place:**
- Nancy Marlowe (USA)

TOP 210: ⭐⭐⭐
- **In 207th Place:**
- Terri James (USA)
- **In 210th Place:**
- Andrew Anderson (USA)

TOP 215: ⭐⭐⭐
- **In 211th Place:**
- Brenda Tenerelli (USA)
- **In 212th Place:**
- Carole Lynne (USA)
- **In 213th Place:**
- Catherine Roller (USA)
- **In 214th Place:**
- Darren Green (USA)
- **In 215th Place:**
- Dawn Bothie (USA)

TOP 220: ⭐⭐⭐
- **In 216th Place:**
- Derek Calibre (USA)
- **In 217th Place:**
- Destiny (USA)
- **In 2168th Place:**
- Elizabeth Wissbaum (USA)
- **In 219th Place:**
- Isabelle Dawes (USA)
- **In 220th Place:**
- Kelli Faulkner (USA)

TOP 225: ⭐⭐⭐
- **In 221th Place:**
- Legina Waters Smith (USA)
- **In 223rd Place:**
- Love Grado (USA)
- **In 224th Place:**
- Lydia DiVincenzo (USA)

- **In 225th Place:**
- Matt Fraser (USA)

TOP 230: ⭐⭐⭐
- **In 226th Place:**
- Matina (USA)
- **In 227th Place:**
- Michelle Gilhouse (USA)
- **In 228th Place:**
- Nancy Feranec (USA)
- **In 229th Place:**
- Peter Chef (USA)
- **In 230th Place:**
- Peter J. Serraino (USA)

TOP 235: ⭐⭐⭐
- **In 231st Place:**
- Phil Jordan (USA)
- **In 232nd Place:**
- Rachel Norway (USA)
- **In 234th Place:**
- Rick Waid (USA)
- **In 235th Place:**
- Robert Bourassa (USA)

TOP 240: ⭐⭐⭐
- **In 236th Place:**
- Rosalee Karls (USA)
- **In 237th Place:**
- Ryan Smith (USA)
- **In 238th Place:**
- Susan Rowlen (USA)
- **In 239th Place:**
- Tori Allah (USA)
- **In 240th Place:**
- Ursula Kalin (USA)

TOP 245: ⭐⭐⭐
- **In 241st Place:**
- Venus Andrecht (USA)
- **In 242nd Place:**
- Vianne Higgins (USA)
- **In 243rd Place:**
- Walter Zajac (USA)
- **In 244th Place:**
- Angela Kruszka (USA)
- **In 245th Place:**
- Anthony Morgan (USA)

TOP 250: ⭐⭐⭐
- **In 246th Place:**
- Arice Miranda (USA)
- **In 247th Place:**
- Barbara Delong (USA)
- **In 248th Place:**
- Bonnie Albers (USA)
- **In 249th Place:**
- Carolyn Myss (USA)
- **In 250th Place:**
- Chanda Reaves (USA)

TOP 255: ⭐⭐⭐
- **In 251st Place:**
- Christina Nelson (USA
- **In 252nd Place:**
- Christine Corda (USA)
- **In 253rd Place:**
- Claire Braddock (USA)
- **In 254th Place:**
- Dana Plant (USA)
- **In 255th Place:**
- Delia Yeager (USA)

TOP 260: ⭐⭐⭐
- **In 256th Place:**

- Dolores Cardelucci (USA)
- **In 257th Place:**
- Dorothy Morgan (USA)
- **In 258th Place:**
- **In 260th Place:**
- Gemini Rose (USA)

TOP 265: ⭐⭐⭐
- **In 261st Place:**
- Gerta Lestock (USA)
- **In 262nd Place:**
- James Demos (USA)
- **In 265th Place:**
- Jeremie Leischner (USA)

TOP 270: ⭐⭐⭐
- **In 266th Place:**
- Jill Dahne (USA)
- **In 267th Place:**
- Jonna Kay Carlson (USA)
- **In 268th Place:**
- Joshua John (USA)
- **In 269th Place:**
- Karleen Heller (USA)
- **In 270th Place:**
- Kay Jacobs (USA)

TOP 275: ⭐⭐⭐
- **In 271st Place:**
- Laura Alden Kamm (USA)
- **In 272nd Place:**
- Marcy Currier (USA)
- **In 273rd Place:**
- Matthew Brandau (USA)
- **In 274th Place:**
- Paddy Chaver (USA)

TOP 280: ⭐⭐⭐

112

- **In 278th Place:**
- Robyn Fritz (USA)
- **In 279th Place:**
- Rosalee Karls (USA)
- **In 280th Place:**
- Saundra Greene (USA)

TOP 285: ⭐⭐⭐
- **In 281st Place:**
- Sheena Metal (USA)
- **In 282nd Place:**
- Sondra Sneed (USA)
- **In 284th Place:**
- Stan Kestrel (USA)
- **In 285th Place:**
- Ula Yule (USA)

TOP 290: ⭐⭐⭐
- **In 287th Place:**
- Victoria Granados (USA)
- **In 290th Place:**
- Amy Cavanaugh (USA)

TOP 295: ⭐⭐⭐
- **In 291st Place:**
- Angie Mitchell (USA)
- **In 292nd Place:**
- Anthony Morgann (USA)
- **In 293rd Place:**
- Barbara DeLong (USA)
- **In 294th Place:**
- Brandy Marie Miller (USA)
- **In 295th Place:**
- Bree Peltier (USA)

TOP 300: ⭐⭐⭐

- **In 296th Place:**
- Brenda Tenerelli (USA)
- **In 297th Place:**
- Candy Odonnell (USA)
- **In 298th Place:**
- Cari Roy (USA)
- **In 299th Place:**
- Celia Caulfield (USA)
- **In 300th Place:**
- Chris White (USA)

TOP 305: ⭐⭐⭐

- **In 302nd Place:**
- Cindy Greene (USA)
- **In 303rd Place:**
- Claire Candy Hough (USA)
- **In 305th Place:**
- Corrine DeWinter (USA)

TOP 310: ⭐⭐⭐

- **In 306th Place:**
- Danielle Mackinnon (USA)
- **In 308th Place:**
- Dawn Mystic Haven (USA)
- **In 309th Place:**
- DC Love (USA)
- **In 310th Place:**
- Diana Richardson (USA)

TOP 315: ⭐⭐⭐

- **In 311th Place:**
- Diane Hamilton (USA)
- **In 312th Place:**
- Echo Bodine (USA)
- **In 313th Place:**
- Eileen Boettcher (USA)
- **In 314th Place:**

- Elisjah Anderzen (USA)

TOP 320: ⭐⭐⭐
- **In 316th Place:**
- Eric Glyn (USA)
- **In 318th Place:**
- Feebee McIntyre (USA)
- **In 319th Place:**
- Heather Coleman-Ibrahim (USA)
- **In 320th Place:**
- Jean Salch (USA)

TOP 325: ⭐⭐⭐
- **In 321stPlace:**
- Jeanne Clock (USA)
- **In 322nd Place:**
- Kate Sitka (USA)
- **In 323rd Place:**
- Ken Morris (USA)
- **In 324th Place:**
- Kristen Lavespere (USA)
- **In 325th Place:**
- Lee Papa (USA)

TOP 330: ⭐⭐⭐
- **In 326th Place:**
- Leslie Hinojosa (USA)
- **In 327th Place:**
- Lori Connell (USA)
- **In 328th Place:**
- Lori Green-Connell (USA)
- **In 329th Place:**
- Lynn Van-Praagh-Gratton (USA)

TOP 335: ⭐⭐⭐
- **In 333rd Place:**

- Mike Loop (USA)
- **In 334th Place:**
- Misty Sevy (USA)

TOP 340: ⭐⭐⭐
- **In 337th Place:**
- Pamela Cummins (USA)
- **In 338th Place:**
- Patrick De Haan (USA)
- **In 339th Place:**
- Peg Jones (USA)
- **In 340th Place:**
- Peter Psychic Chef (USA)

TOP 345: ⭐⭐⭐
- **In 341st Place:**
- Quinton Carlson (USA)
- **In 342nd Place:**
- Rachel Marie (USA)
- **In 343rd Place:**
- Renee Richards (USA)
- **In 344th Place:**
- Robert F. Burke (USA)

TOP 350: ⭐⭐⭐
- **In 346th Place:**
- Rochelle Sparrow (USA)
- **In 347th Place:**
- Sandra Greene (USA)
- **In 348th Place:**
- Sarah LaBrie (USA)
- **In 349th Place:**
- Sarah McCoy (USA)

TOP 355: ⭐⭐⭐
- **In 351st Place:**
- Shanon Corkins (USA)
- **In 352nd Place:**

- Shelley Duffy (USA)
- **In 353rd Place:**
- Solana (USA)
- **In 354th Place:**
- Sprinkles Nixon (USA)
- **In 355th Place:**
- Sue Dalimonte (USA)

TOP 360: ⭐⭐⭐

- **In 356th Place:**
- Sue Rae (USA)
- **In 357th Place:**
- Susan Sanderford (USA)
- **In 359th Place:**
- Timitha Bryan (USA)
- **In 360th Place:**
- Jeannine G Wand (USA)

TOP 365: ⭐⭐⭐

- **In 361st Place:**
- Smirti Mukherjee (USA)
- **In 362nd Place:**
- Kenneth Bentley (USA)
- **In 363rd Place:**
- Anna Robles Simon (USA)
- Roy Worley (USA)

NOTE: Names of lightworkers who have received less than 3 votes were deleted. (Approximately 1900 names)

BEST PSYCHICS IN THE UNITED STATES

TOP 5 PSYCHICS IN THE UNITED STATES IN THIS RANK ORDER: ★★★★★
- **In 1st Place:**
- Patti Negri
- **In 2nd Place:**
- Jennifer Wallens

- Michelle Whitedove
- **In 3rd Place:**
- Tracy Lee Nash
- Sunhee and Chinhee Park
- **In 4th Place:**
- Suzanne Grace
- **In 5th Place:**
- Micki Dahne
- Concetta Bertoldi

TOP 10 PSYCHICS IN THE UNITED STATES IN THIS RANK ORDER: ★★★★★

- **In 6th Place:**
- Jessicca Cannon Haas
- Allison Hayes
- **In 7th Place:**
- Vickie Gay
- **In 8th Place:**
- Dianne Hiller
- **In 9th Place:**
- Lorraine Roe
- **In 10th Place:**
- Melissa Stamps

TOP 15 PSYCHICS IN THE UNITED STATES IN THIS RANK ORDER: ★★★★★

- **In 11th Place:**
- Melissa Berman
- **In 12th Place:**
- Colette Baron-Reid
- **In 13th Place:**
- Joyce Keller
- **In 14th Place:**
- Judy Hevenly
- **In 15th Place:**
- Kimberly Ward
- Nicki Bonfilio

TOP 20 PSYCHICS IN THE UNITED STATES IN THIS RANK ORDER: ★★★★★

- **In 16th Place:**
- Greta Alexander
- **In 16th Place:**
- Roxanne Elizabeth Usleman
- **In 18th Place:**
- Frank Andrews
- **In 19th Place:**
- Daved Beck
- **In 20th Place:**
- PennyC

TOP 25 PSYCHICS IN THE UNITED STATES IN THIS RANK ORDER: ★★★★★

- **In 21th Place:**
- Dena Flanagan
- **In 22nd Place:**
- John Cappello
- **In 23rd Place:**
- Sherie Hurd Roufusse
- **In 24th Place:**
- John Harricharan
- **In 25th Place:**
- Stacey Wolf-James

TOP 30 PSYCHICS IN THE UNITED STATES IN THIS RANK ORDER: ★★★★★

- **In 26th Place:**
- Kim Russo
- **In 27th Place:**
- Carmen Harra, PhD
- **In 28th Place:**
- Elizabeth Joyce
- **In 29th Place:**
- Laura Mendelsohn
- **In 30th Place:**
- Linda Lauren

TOP 35 PSYCHICS IN THE UNITED STATES IN THIS
RANK ORDER: ★★★★★

- **In 31st Place:**
- Kim Russo
- **In 32nd Place:**
- Jennifer Shackford
- **In 33rd Place:**
- Karen Page
- **In 34th Place:**
- Krzysztof "Kris" Chmielewski
- **In 35th Place:**
- Allison Dubois

TOP 40 PSYCHICS IN THE UNITED STATES IN THIS
RANK ORDER: ★★★★★

- **In 36th Place:**
- Jethro Smith
- **In 37th Place:**
- Doreen Virtue
- **In 38th Place:**
- Jake Samoyedny
- **In 39th Place:**
- James Van Praagh
- **In 40th Place:**
- Lisa Williams

TOP 45 PSYCHICS IN THE UNITED STATES IN THIS
RANK ORDER: ★★★★★

- **In 41st Place:**
- John Holland
- **In 42nd Place:**
- Mary Ennis
- **In 43rd Place:**
- Rosemary Altea
- **In 44th Place:**
- Jamie Butler
- **In 45th Place:**
- Char Margolis

TOP 50 PSYCHICS IN THE UNITED STATES IN THIS RANK ORDER: ★★★★★

- **In 46th Place:**
- Litany Burns
- **In 47th Place:**
- Janine Regan Sinclair
- **In 48th Place:**
- Mary T. Browne
- **In 49th Place:**
- Patricia Mischell
- **In 50th Place:**

TOP 55 PSYCHICS IN THE UNITED STATES IN THIS RANK ORDER: ★★★★★

- **In 51st Place:**
- Kathlyn Rhea
- **In 52nd Place:**
- Carla Baron
- **In 53rd Place:**
- Chip Coffey
- **In 54th Place:**
- Patricia Masters
- **In 55th Place:**
- Stephen Robinson

TOP 60 PSYCHICS IN THE UNITED STATES IN THIS RANK ORDER: ★★★★★

- **In 56th Place:**
- Karina Vorosilova
- **In 57th Place:**
- Joanne Gerber
- **In 58th Place:**
- Lorraine Lush
- **In 59th Place:**
- Lori Karras
- **In 60th Place:**

- Claudia Johnson

TOP 65 PSYCHICS IN THE UNITED STATES IN THIS RANK ORDER: ★★★★★
- **In 61st Place:**
- Keli Michaels
- **In 62nd Place:**
- Tarah Harper
- **In 63rd Place:**
- Barbara Mackey
- **In 64th Place:**
- Joan Bunyan
- **In 65th Place:**
- Lydia Clar

TOP 70 PSYCHICS IN THE UNITED STATES IN THIS RANK ORDER: ★★★★★
- **In 66th Place:**
- Sharon Kissane
- **In 67th Place:**
- John Edward
- **In 68th Place:**
- Noreen Renier
- **In 69th Place:**
- Nancy Myer
- **In 70th Place:**
- Abby Rose Newman

TOP 75 PSYCHICS IN THE UNITED STATES IN THIS RANK ORDER: ★★★★★
- **In 71st Place:**
- Linda Salvin, Ph.D
- **In 72nd Place:**
- Andrew Brewer
- **In 73rdPlace:**
- Sandra Nemet

- **In 74th Place:**
- Helene Frisch
- **In 75th Place:**
- Terry and Linda Jamison

TOP 80 PSYCHICS IN THE UNITED STATES IN THIS RANK ORDER: ★★★★★

- **In 76th Place:**
- Maya Britan
- **In 77th Place:**
- Dorothy Allyson
- **In 78th Place:**
- Adrienne Miles
- **In 79th Place:**
- Bee Herz
- **In 80th Place:**
- Pam Coronado

TOP 85 PSYCHICS IN THE UNITED STATES IN THIS RANK ORDER: ★★★★★

- **In 81st Place:**
- Thomas John
- **In 82nd Place:**
- Chris Avery Cole
- **In 83rd Place:**
- Theresa Caputo
- **In 84th Place:**
- Marla Phillips
- **In 85th Place:**
- Ashlei Yatron

TOP 90 PSYCHICS IN THE UNITED STATES IN THIS RANK ORDER: ★★★★

- **In 86th Place:**
- Belle Salisbury
- **In 87th Place:**
- Sharon Pugh

- **In 88th Place:**
- Linda Irwin
- **In 89th Place:**
- Lynn Bleasdale
- **In 90th Place:**
- Dawn Short

TOP 95 PSYCHICS IN THE UNITED STATES IN THIS RANK ORDER:

- **In 91st Place:**
- Rachel Marie
- **In 92nd Place:**
- Steven Harvey
- **In 93rd Place:**
- Sue Raye
- **In 94thPlace:**
- Gary Wimmer
- **In 95th Place:**
- Peg Jones

TOP 100 PSYCHICS IN THE UNITED STATES IN THIS RANK ORDER:

- **In 96th Place:**
- Amelia Armstrong
- **In 97th Place:**
- Betsy Cohen
- **In 98th Place:**
- Kelly Coulter
- **In 99th Place:**
- Pamela Cushman
- **In 100th Place:**
- Cassandra Larsen

TOP 105 PSYCHICS IN THE UNITED STATES IN THIS RANK ORDER:

- **In 101st Place:**
- Elizabeth Baron

- **In 102nd Place:**
- Nancy Bradley
- **In 103rd Place:**
- Laura Jackson
- **In 104th Place:**
- Jamie Clark
- **In 105th Place:**
- Jan Drake Bakke

TOP 110 PSYCHICS IN THE UNITED STATES IN THIS RANK ORDER:

- **In 106th Place:**
- Sally Brustowicz
- **In 107th Place:**
- Vicki L. Robinson
- **In 108th Place:**
- Jeannine G Wand
- **In 109th Place:**
- Kenneth Bentley
- **In 110th Place:**
- Anna Robles Simon (USA)

NOTE: Names of lightworkers who have received less than 3 votes were deleted. (Approximately 677 names)

*** *** ***

Last Year's Best Psychics in the United States: Listing by Rank and Number of Votes.

TOP 5 IN THE UNITED STATES: 5 STARS RATING

#1: 2405 votes. Patti Negri. Last year's rank: Number 3 in the world and Number 1 in the United States.

#2: 2001 votes. Jennifer Wallens. Last year's rank: Number 34 in the world.

#3: 1786 votes. Michelle Whitedove. Last year's rank: Number 17 in the world and Number 10 in the United States.

#3: 1786 votes. Chinhee & Sunhee Park. Last year's rank: Number 3 in the world and Number 1 in the United States.

#4: 1407 votes: Suzanne Grace. Last year's rank: Number 60 in the world.

#5: 1406 votes. Kimberly Ward.

TOP 10 IN THE UNITED STATES: 5 STARS RATING

#6: 912 votes. Shannon Leischner. Last year's rank: Number 60 in the world

#6: 912 votes. Linda Salvin, Ph.D. Last year's rank: Number 4 in the world and Number 2 in the United States.

#7: 564 votes. Allison Hayes. Last year's rank: Number 7 in the world, and Number 1 in the world in 2011.

#7: 564 votes. Shellee Halle. Last year's rank: Number 65 in the world. 2011-2012 America's 2nd best psychic, and America's Most Famous and Popular Psychic. Rank #1.

#7: 564 votes. Belle Salisbury. Last year's rank: Number 68 in the world.

#8: 527 votes. John Holland. Last year's rank: Number 36 in the world.

#9: 400 votes. Jessica Cannon Haas. Last year's rank: Number 57 in the world.

#10: 360 votes. Jethro Smith. Last year's rank: Number 55 in the world.
#10: 360 votes. Lorie Johnson.
 #10: 317 votes. Sherrie Hurd-Roufosse.

TOP 15 IN THE UNITED STATES: 4 STARS RATING

#11: 340 votes. Karina Voroshilova.
#12: 300 votes. Amelia Pisano Scozzari (Canada/USA
#13: 292 votes. Terry and Linda Jamison.
#13: 292 votes. Chip Coffey (USA). World Rank: 85th Place in the world.
#14: 180 votes. Daved Beck.
#15: 161 votes. Doreen Virtue. Last year's rank: Number 12 in the world. 161 votes. Van Doren Figueredo.

TOP 20 IN THE UNITED STATES: 4 STARS RATING

#16: 160 votes. Keli Michaels. Last year's rank: Number 82 in the world.
#17: 159 votes. Micki Dahne. Last year's rank: Number 28 in the world.
#18: 159 votes. PennyC. Last year's rank: Number 29 in the world.
#19: 154 votes. Cassandra Larsen
#20: 91 votes. James Van Praagh.
#20: 91 votes. Char Margolis. Last year's rank: Number 13 in the world.

TOP 25 IN THE UNITED STATES: 3 STARS RATING

#21: 88 votes. Jamie Clark. Last year's rank: Number 89 in the world.
#22: 87 votes. Carla Baron. Last year's rank: Number 67 in the world.
#23: 82 votes. Lisa Williams. Last year's rank: Number 25 in the world and Number 17 in the United States.

#23: 82 votes. Barbara Mackey. Last year's rank: Number 74 in the world and Number 17 in the United States.

#23: 82 votes. Rosemary Altea. Last year's rank: Number 50 in the world

#24: 81 votes. John Edward. Last year's rank: Number 51 in the world.

#25: 79 votes. Noreen Renier. Last year's rank: Number 24 in the world.

TOP 30 IN THE UNITED STATES: 3 STARS RATING

#26: 78 votes. Allison Dubois. Last year's rank: Number 8 in the world.

#26: 78 votes. Dawn Short. Last year's rank: Number 23 in the world.

#26: 78 votes. Gayle Kirk. Last year's rank: Number 77 in the world.

#27: 77 votes. Sandra Nemet.

#28: 76 votes. Mary Ennis. Last year's rank: Number 18 in the world.

#28: 76 votes. Stephen Robinson. Last year's rank: Number 100 in the world.

#28: 76 votes. Sharon Kissane. Last year's rank: Number 38 in the world.

#29: 75 votes. Melissa Stamps. Last year's rank: Number 76 in the world.

#29: 75 votes. Kathlyn Rhea. Last year's rank: Number 23 in the world and Number 10 in the United States.

#29: 75 votes. Andrew Brewer. Last year's rank: Number 70 in the world.

#30: 74 votes. Joan Bunyan. Last year's rank: Number 79 in the world.

TOP 35 IN THE UNITED STATES: 3 STARS RATING

#31: 72 votes. Joanne Gerber. Last year's rank: Number 97 in the world.

#32: 71 votes. Matthew Brandau.

#33: 70 votes. Sharon Pugh. Last year's rank: Number 74 in the world.

#34: 69 votes. Ingo Swann. Last year's rank: Number 89 in the world.

#35: 68 votes. Lori Karras. Last year's rank: Number 90 in the world.

TOP 40 IN THE UNITED STATES: 2 STARS RATING

#36: 67 votes. Lydia Clar. Last year's rank: Number 90 in the world.

#37: 66 votes. Thomas John. Last year's rank: Number 91 in the world.

#37: 66 votes. Nancy Myer. Last year's rank: Number 22 in the world.

#38: 65 votes. Adrienne Miles

#38: 65 votes. Dorothy Allyson. Last year's rank: Number 20 in the world.

#39: 64 votes. Matt Fraser.

#40: 63 votes. Sylvia Browne. Last year's rank: Number 37 in the world.

TOP 45 IN THE UNITED STATES: 2 STARS RATING

- #41: 62 votes. Peter J. Serraino. Last year's rank: Number 77 in the world.
- #42: 61 votes. Kelly Coulter. Last year's rank: Number 92 in the world.
- #43: 60 votes. Helene Frisch. Last year's rank: Number 73 in the world.
- #44: 59 votes. Marla Phillips. Last year's rank: Number 66 in the world.
- #44: 59 votes. Amelia Armstrong.
- #45: 58 votes. Michelle Belanger.
- #45: 58 votes. Nancy Bradley. Last year's rank: Number 75 in the world.

TOP 50 IN THE UNITED STATES: 2 STARS RATING

- #46: 57 votes. Amanda Hufford
- #47: 56 votes. Carrie-Anne Hartley Silkowski.

- #47: 56 votes. Amanda Hufford.
- #48: 55 votes. Elizabeth Baron. Last year's rank: Number 81 in the world.
- #48: 55 votes. Donna McGrath.
- #49: 54 votes. Joan Donahue. Last year's rank: Number 93 in the world.
- #50: 53 votes. Kelly MacLeod. Last year's rank: Number 94 in the world.

TOP 55 IN THE UNITED STATES: 2 STARS RATING

- #51: 50 votes. Joseph Tittlel
- #52: 49 votes. Brian Hunter.
- #53: 48 votes. Michelle Beltran.
- #54: 47 votes. Sarah White. Last year's rank: Number 95 in the world.
- #55: 46 votes. Zoe McDonald. Last year's rank: Number 96 in the world.

TOP 60 IN THE UNITED STATES: 1 STAR RATING

- #56: 45 votes. Fahrusha. Last year's rank: Number 96 in the world.
- #57: 44 votes. Tracy Neeley. Last year's rank: Number 70 in the world.
- #58: 43 votes. Angela Heil
- #59: 42 votes. Nikki Steward.
- #60: 41 votes. Abby Star Lippit.
- #60: 41 votes. Ada May Brown.

TOP 65 IN THE UNITED STATES: 1 STAR RATING

- #61: 39 votes. Abby Rose Newman.
- #62: 38 votes. Lorraine Roe. Last year's rank: Number 55 in the world.
- #62: 38 votes. Alyssia Terenzi.
- #62: 38 votes. Steven Lloyd-Johnson.
- #63: 36 votes. Shirlee Teabo.
- #64: 35 votes. Adam Doporto.

- #64: 35 votes. Aurora Rose aka Stephanie Stinnett. Last year's rank: Number 72 in the world.
- #65: 34 votes. Tara Night.

TOP 70 IN THE UNITED STATES: 1 STAR RATING

- #66: 33 votes. Valerie Morrison.
- #66: 33 votes. Beth Carpenter.
- #67: 32 votes. Veronica Figueroa.
- #68: 31 votes. Becky Blanco.
- #69: 30 votes. Vicki L. Robinson.
- #70: 29 votes. Tina Saelee (USA/Thailand). Last year's rank: Number 50 in the world.
- #70: 29 votes. Jerry Yusko.
- #70: 29 votes. Bella Mason.

TOP 75 IN THE UNITED STATES: 1 STAR RATING

- #71: 28 votes. Justin Chase Mullins. Last year's rank: Number 35 in the world.
- #71: 28 votes. Sandy Anastasi.
- #71: 28 votes. Irene Hope Burke.
- #72: 27 votes. Wendy Piepenburg.
- #72: 27 votes. Barbara Delozier.
- #73: 25 votes. Rubbie Salinas aka Rubbizfire.
- #73: 25 votes. Sunny Wang.
- #74: 25 votes. Jennifer Shackford.
- #74: 25 votes. Lorraine Roe. Last year's rank: Number 55 in the world.
- #75: 24 votes. Silvana Fillmore. Last year's rank: Number 99 in the world.
- #75: 24 votes. Sandra Lynn Sparks.

TOP 80 IN THE UNITED STATES: 1 STAR RATING

- #76: 23 votes. Melissa Berman.

- #77: 23 votes. Greta Alexander. Last year's rank: Number 17 in the world and Number 13 in the United States.
- #78: 21 votes. Tiffany Michelle Bil. Last year's rank: Number 15 in the world.
- #79: 20 votes. Mary Occhino. Last year's rank: Number 27 in the world.
- #79: 20 votes. Anne Diedre Smith.
- #80: 19 votes. Cynthia Segal. Last year's rank: Number 72 in the world.

TOP 85 IN THE UNITED STATES: 1 STAR RATING

- #81: 18 votes. Donna Seebo.
- #82: 17 votes. Adela Linsalata.
- #83: 16 votes. Stacey Wolf.
- #84: 16 votes. Leo Brown.
- #84: 16 votes. Dena Flanagan.
- #85: 15 votes. Zenobia Simmons.
- #85: 15 votes. Pam Heslin.

TOP 90 IN THE UNITED STATES: 1 STAR RATING

- #86: 14 votes. George Withers.
- #86: 14 votes. Barrie John.
- #87: 12 votes. Belinda Bentley.
- #87: 12 votes. Leeza Cannon.
- #88: 11 votes. April Ashbrook.
- #88: 11 votes. Cris Avery Cole.
- #89: 11 votes. Barbara Norcross.
- #90: 9 votes: Amy Cavanaugh. Last year's rank: Number 75 in the world.

TOP 95 IN THE UNITED STATES: 1 STAR RATING

- #91: 8 votes. William Deep.
- #91: 8 votes. Jan Drake Bakke.

- #91: 8 votes. Pam Coronado. Last year's rank: Number 40 in the world.
- #92: 7 votes. Angela Lusk.
- #93: 6 votes. Tracy Lee Nash. Last year's rank: Number 16 in the world.
- #94: 5 votes. Francine Milano.
- #94: 5 votes. Gary Wimmer.
- #95: 4 votes. Kristen Leona.
- #95: 4 votes. Bee Herz.
- #95: 4 votes. Celeste Corkins. Last year's rank: Number 86 in the world.
- #95: 4 votes. Sarina St. John.
- #95: 4 votes. Robert Rodriguez.

OTHERS

- #96: 3 votes. Doyle Ward.
- #96: 3 votes. Kelli Faulkner.
- #96: 2 votes. Harriette Knight.
- #96: 2 votes. Jonna Kay Carlson.
- #96: 2 votes. Gerta Lestock.
- #97: 1 vote. Angela Bixby.
- #97: 1 vote. Kay Jacobs.
- #97: 1 vote. Anthony Morgann.
- #97: 1 vote. Arice Miranda.
- #97: 1 vote. Astrid.
- #97: 1 vote. Barbara Delong.
- #97: 1 vote. Beau Salinas Jr.
- #97: 1 vote. Bonnie Albers.
- #97: 1 vote. Catherine Roller.
- #97: 1 vote. Christa Urban.
- #97: 1 vote. Christine Corda.
- #97: 1 vote. Coryelle Kramer.
- #97: 1 vote. Delia Yeager.
- #97: 1 vote. Dolores Cardelucci.
- #97: 1 vote. Dorothy Morgan.
- #97: 1 vote. Elizabeth Wissbaum.
- #97: 1 vote. Gemini Rose.
- #97: 1 vote. Georgia Cuningham.

- #97: 1 vote. Georgia Marantos, MD.
- #97: 1 vote. Jamie Butler.
- #97: 1 vote. Jane Borowski.
- #97: 1 vote. Janine Regan Sinclair.
- #97: 1 vote. Jeremie Leischner.
- #97: 1 vote. Jill Dahne.
- #97: 1 vote. Joshua John.
- #97: 1 vote. Kristen Lavespere.
- #97: 1 vote. Linda Irwin.
- #97: 1 vote. Linda Jolley.
- #97: 1 vote. Marcy Currier.
- #97: 1 vote. Mike Loop. Last year's rank: Number 71 in the world.
- #97: 1 vote. Paddy Chaver.
- #97: 1 vote. Pamela Cummins.
- #97: 1 vote. Peg Jones.
- #97: 1 vote. Peter Chef.
- #97: 1 vote. Rick Waid.
- #97: 1 vote. Robyn Fritz.
- #97: 1 vote. Rosalee Karls.
- #97: 1 vote. Ryan Smith.
- #97: 1 vote. Sarah LaBrie. Last year's rank: Number 68 in the world.
- #97: 1 vote. Sarah Meredith.
- #97: 1 vote. Sondra Sneed.
- #97: 1 vote. Stan Kestrel.
- #97: 1 vote. Sue Rae.
- #97: 1 vote. Tara Sutphen.
- #97: 1 vote. Terri James.
- #97: 1 vote. Tori Allah.
- #97: 1 vote. Ula Yule.
- #97: 1 vote. Ursula Kalin.
- #97: 1 vote. Vianne Higgins.
- #97: 1 vote. William Constantine. Last year's rank: Number 14 in the world.
- #97: 1 vote. Saundra Greene.
- #97: 1 vote. Chanda Reaves.
- #97: 1 vote. Sally Brustowicz.
- #97: 1 vote. Shanon Corkins.

- #97: 1 vote. Venus Andrecht.
- #97: 1 vote. Dawn Bothie.
- #97: 1 vote. Laura Alden Kamm.
- #97: 1 vote. Carol Ritberger.
- #97: 1 vote. Carolyn Myss.
- #97: 1 vote. Mariah Crawford.
- #97: 1 vote. Isabelle Dawes.
- #97: 1 vote. Candy Odonnell.
- #97: 1 vote. Pamela Cushman.
- #97: 1 vote. Lee Papa.
- #97: 1 vote. James Demos.
- #97: 1 vote. Ashley Riley.
- #97: 1 vote. Darren Green.
- #97: 1 vote. Christina Nelson.

*** *** ***

BEST ANGEL READERS, ANGEL PSYCHICS, ANGEL CHANNEL IN THE UNITED STATES

In Alphabetical Order:

A

- Angela Bixbi (USA)
- Artie Hoffman (USA)

B

- Barbara Anderson (USA)
- Brianna Brooks (USA)

C

- Cheryl Murphy (USA)
- Corbie Mitleid, Reverend (USA)

D

- Denise Bennett (USA)
  Doreen Virtue (USA

E

- Elizabeth Barnett (USA)

G

- Ginger Quinlan (USA)
- Gliselda Amarillas-Ramirez (USA)

H

- Heather Valentine (USA)

J

- Jen Prothero (USA)
- Jennifer Shackford (USA)
- Jennifer Shaffer (USA)
- Julie Lynn Rogers (USA)
  Jacque McPherson (USA)

K

- Kathryn Samuelson (USA)

L

- Laura Lyn (USA)
- Lisa Atkinson (USA)
- Lisa Beachy (USA)

M

- Maria Jensen (USA)
- Mariana Cooper (USA)
- Mary Strauss (USA)
- Michelle Whitedove (USA)

N

- Nadia Starella (USA)
- Nancine Meyer (USA)
- Nancy Christie Johansen (USA)
- Noelle Garneau (USA)

P

- PennyC (USA)

R

- Robin (USA)
- Rose Ann Schwab, Ph.D. (USA)

S

- Shannon Leischner (USA)
- Suzanne Grace (USA)

Best Angels Readers, Angels Psychics, Angel Channel
In National Rank Order.

TOP 5: ★★★★★
- · **In 1st Place:**
- · Michelle Whitedove (USA)
- · **In 2nd Place:**
- · Rose Ann Schwab, Ph.D. (USA)
- · Suzanne Grace (USA)
- · **In 3rd Place:**
- · Laura Lyn (USA)
- · **In 4th Place:**
- · Doreen Virtue (USA)
- · **In 5th Place:**
- · Corbie Mitleid, Reverend (USA)

Michelle Whitedove. Rose Ann Schwab, Ph.D.

Suzanne Grace. Laura Lyn.

Doreen Virtue. Corbie Mitleid.

TOP 10: ★★★★★
- **In 6ᵗʰ Place:**
- Jennifer Shaffer (USA)
- **In 7ᵗʰ Place:**
- Briana Brooks (USA)
- **In 8ᵗʰ Place:**
- Jennifer Shackford (USA)

Jennifer Shaffer. Briana Brooks (USA).

Jennifer Shackford.

- **In 9th Place:**
- Shannon Leischner (USA)
- **In 10th Place:**
- PennyC (USA)

TOP 15: ★★★★★

- **In 11th Place:**
- Angela Bixbi (USA)
- **In 12th Place:**
- Noelle Garneau (USA)
- **In 13th Place:**
- Elizabeth Barnett (USA)

Shannon Leischner. PennyC.

143

Angela Bixbi. Noelle Garneau.

Elizabeth Barnett (USA).

- **In 14th Place:**
- Denise Bennett (USA)
- **In 15th Place:**
- Artie Hoffman (USA)

TOP 20: ★★★★★

- **In 16th Place:**
- Barbara Anderson (USA)
- **In 17th Place:**
- Nadia Starella (USA)
- **In 18th Place:**
- Cheryl Murphy (USA)

Denise Bennett. Artie Hoffman.

Nadia Starella. Cheryl Murphy.

- **In 19st Place:**
- Jen Prothero (USA)
- **In 20th Place:**
- Heather Valentine (USA)

TOP 25:

- **In 21st Place:**
- Nancine Meyer (USA)
- **In 22nd Place:**
- Nancy Christie Johansen (USA)
- **In 23rd Place:**
- Mariana Cooper (USA)

- **In 24th Place:**
- Mary Strauss (USA)
- **In 25th Place:**
- Lisa Atkinson (USA)

TOP 30: ★★★★

- **In 26th Place:**
- Robin (USA)
- **In 27th Place:**
- Maria Jensen (USA)
- **In 28th Place:**
- Julie Lynn Rogers (USA)
- **In 29th Place:**
- Ginger Quinlan (USA)
- **In 30th Place:**
- Kathryn Samuelson (USA)

TOP 35: ★★★★

- **In 31st Place:**
- Lisa Beachy (USA)
- **In 32nd Place:**
- Gliselda Amarillas-Ramirez (USA)
- **In 33rd Place:**
- Jacque McPherson (USA)

***   ***   ***

BEST TAROT READERS IN THE UNITED STATES

Tarot Reader Category by Alphabetical Order.

A

- Andy Young (USA)
- Angela Kruszka (USA)
- Angela Lucy (USA)

C

- Chris White (USA)
- Cindy Greene (USA)
- Crimson Kitty (USA)

D

- Diane Williams (USA)

F

- FeeBee McIntyre (USA)
- Frank Andrews (USA)

J

- Jessie Caldwell (USA)
- Jethro Smith (USA)
- Joy Rilling (USA)

K

- Karen Cote (USA)
- Karina Voroshilova (USA)
- Kaye Gordon (USA)
- Krzysztof "Kris" Chmielewski (USA)

L

- Laura Colavito-Agosta (USA)
- Lynne Taylor (USA)
- Lynsi Wood (USA)

M

- Marcy Currier (USA)

P

- Patti Negri (USA)

R

- Robert Rodriguez (USA)

S

- Solana (USA)
- Sue Raye (USA)

T

- Tina Carey (USA)

Y

- Yolanda Billings (USA)

By national rank order. 5 Stars:

TOP5: ★★★★★
- **In 1st Place:**
- Patti Negri
- **In 2nd Place:**
- Yolanda Billings
- **In 3rd Place:**
- Jethro Smith
- **In 4th Place:**
- Frank Andrews

Patti Negri. Krysztof Chmielewski.

Yolanda Billings. Jethro Smith.

Frank Andrews.

- **In 5th Place:**
- Karina Voroshilova

TOP10: ★★★★★
- **In 6th Place:**
- Angela Kruszka
- **In 7th Place:**
- Robert Rodriguez
- **In 8th Place:**
- Andy Young
- **In 9th Place:**
- Angela Lucy
- **In 10th Place:**
- Crimson Kitty

TOP 15 : ★★★★★
- **In 11th Place:**
- Laura Colavito-Agosta
- **In 12th Place:**
- Diane Williams
- **In 13th Place:**
- Joy Rilling
- **In 14th Place:**
- Tina Carey
- **In 15th Place:**
- Lynsi Wood

TOP 20: ★★★★★
- **In 16th Place:**
- Chris White
- **In 17th Place:**
- Cindy Greene
- **In 18th Place:**
- FeeBee McIntyre
- **In 19th Place:**
- Jessie Caldwell
- **In 20th Place:**
- Karen Cote

TOP 25: ★★★★★
- **In 21st Place:**
- Kaye Gordon
- **In 22nd Place:**
- Marcy Currier

*** *** ***

BEST HEALERS IN THE UNITED STATES
By Alphabetical Order.

A

- Alexandra Juliani
- Amy Cavanaugh
- Anthony Morgann
- Ashley Riley

B

- Barbara Brennan
- Benjamin Spock, MD

C

- Carol Ritberger
- Carolyn B. Coleridge, MSW, LCSW
- Carolyn Myss
- Celia Caulfield
- Charles Lightwalker
- Chef Sessy
- Claudia Johnson
- Collette Baron Reid
- Crista Sokolow

D

- DC Love
- Dean Kraft
- Deepak Chopra, MD (India/USA)
- Dena Flanagan
- Diane Williams
- Dina Vitantonio
- Dolores Krieger, RN, Ph.D.

E

- Eileen Boettcher
- Elisa Medhus
- Elisjah Anderzen

G

- Gabriela Castillo

I

- Issam Nemeh, MD

J

- Jack Gray
- Janet Bowerman
- Janine Regan Sinclair
- Jean Salch
- Jeannine G Wand
- Jennifer Shaffer
- Jethro Smith
- Johanna Morgan, MA, CHT

K

- Kay Jacobs
- Kelly Coulter
- Krzysztof "Kris" Chmielewski

L

- Laura Alden Kamm
- Lee Papa
- Lori Coviello
- Lisa Campion
- Lori Green Connell
- Lorie Johnson

M

- Martha Piesco Hoff

O

- Oktobre Taylor

P

- Pam Ragland

R

- Robert Rodriguez
- Roger Laborde
- Roger Nobles
- Rosalyn Bruyere, DD

S

- Sarah West
- Solana
- Steven Weiss, MD

T

- Tarah Harper
- Tina Saelee (USA/Thailand)
- Trilby Johnson

By national Rank Order. 5 and 4 Stars:

TOP 5 HEALERS IN THE US : ★★★★★
- **In 1st Place:**
- Carolyn Myss
- **In 7th Place:**
- Johanna Morgan, MA, CHT
- **In 2nd Place:**

- Barbara Brennan
- Lisa Campion
- **In 3rd Place:**
- Rosalyn Bruyere, DD
- **In 4th Place:**
- Steven Weiss, MD
- **In 5th Place:**
- Dean Kraft

TOP 10 HEALERS IN THE US: ★★★★★
- **In 6th Place:**
- Jack Gray
- **In 7th Place:**
- Alexandra Juliani
- **In 8th Place:**
- Pam Ragland
- **In 9th Place:**
- Martha Piesco Hoff
- **In 10th Place:**
- Issam Nemeh, MD

TOP 15 HEALERS IN THE US : ★★★★★
- **In 11th Place:**
- Carolyn B. Coleridge, MSW, LCSW
- **In 12th Place:**
- Sarah West
- **In 13th Place:**
- Benjamin Spock, MD
- **In 14th Place:**
- Tarah Harper
- **In 15th Place:**
- Roger Laborde

TOP 20 HEALERS IN THE US : ★★★★★
- **In 16th Place:**
- Diane Williams
- **In 17th Place:**
- Krzysztof "Kris" Chmielewski
- **In 18th Place:**
- Claudia Johnson

- **In 19ᵗʰ Place:**
- Jennifer Shaffer
- **In 20ᵗʰ Place:**
- Jethro Smith

TOP 25 HEALERS IN THE US : ★★★★
- **In 21ˢᵗ Place:**
- Dina Vitantonio
- **In 22ⁿᵈ Place:**
- Dena Flanagan
- **In 23ʳᵈ Place:**
- Roger Nobles (USA)
- **In 24ᵗʰ Place:**
- Robert Rodriguez
- **In 25ᵗʰ Place:**
- Amy Cavanaugh

TOP 30 HEALERS IN THE US : ★★★★
- **In 26ᵗʰ Place:**
- Janet Bowerman
- **In 27ᵗʰ Place:**
- Carol Ritberger
- **In 28ᵗʰ Place:**
- Janine Regan Sinclair
- **In 29ᵗʰ Place:**
- Charles Lightwalker
- **In 30ᵗʰ Place:**
- Kelly Coulter

TOP 35 HEALERS IN THE US : ★★★★
- **In 31ˢᵗ Place:**
- Crista Sokolow
- **In 32ⁿᵈ Place:**
- Jean Salch
- **In 33ʳᵈ Place:**
- Anthony Morgann
- **In 34ᵗʰ Place:**
- Ashley Riley
- **In 35ᵗʰ Place:**
- Lori Green Connell

TOP 40 HEALERS IN THE US : ★★★★
- **In 36th Place:**
- Celia Caulfield
- **In 37th Place:**
- Chef Sessy
- **In 38th Place:**
- Collette Baron Reid
- **In 39th Place:**
- DC Love
- **In 40th Place:**
- Elisa Medhus

TOP 45 HEALERS IN THE US: ★★★★
- **In 41st Place:**
- Elisjah Anderzen
- **In 42nd Place:**
- Tina Saelee (USA/Thailand)
- **In 43rd Place:**
- Laura Alden Kamm
- **In 44th Place:**
- Lee Papa
- **In 45th Place:**
- Lori Coviello

TOP 50 HEALERS IN THE US : ★★★★
- **In 46th Place:**
- Oktobre Taylor
- **In 47th Place:**
- Solana
- **In 48th Place:**
- Trilby Johnson
- **In 49th Place:**
- Kay Jacobs
- **In 50th Place:**
- Lorie Johnson

TOP 55 HEALERS IN THE US:

- **In 51ˢᵗ Place:**
- Jeannine G Wand (USA)
- **In 52ⁿᵈ Place:**
- Gabriela Castillo (USA)

Last Year's Best Healers in the United States.

TOP 5: ★★★★★

#1: 9712 votes. Dean Kraft. Last year's rank: Number 3 in the world.

#2: 9549 votes. Roger La Borde. Last year's rank: Number 5 in the world.

#3: 9417 votes. Jack Gray. Last year's rank: Number 4 in the world.

#4: 1071 votes. Alexandra Juliani.

#5: 947 votes. Barbara Brennan. Last year's rank: Number 19 in the world.

TOP 10: ★★★★★

#6: 947 votes. Dr. Steven Weiss, MD. Last year's rank: Number 20 in the world.

#7: 928 votes. Dolores Krieger, RN, Ph.D. Last year's rank: Number 22 in the world.

#8: 911 votes. Carolyn Myss. Last year's rank: Number 22 in the world.

#9: 900 votes. Johanna Morgan, MA, CHT. Last year's rank: Number 23 in the world.

#10: 893 votes. Rosalyn Bruyere, DD. Last year's rank: Number 21 in the world.

TOP 15: ★★★★

#11: 872 votes. Martha Piesco Hoff. Last year's rank: Number 25 in the world.

#12: 870 votes. Issam Nemeh, MD. Last year's rank: Number 16 in the world.

#13: 860 votes. Carolyn B. Coleridge, MSW, LCSW. Last year's rank: Number 24 in the world.

#14: 858 votes. Benjamin Spock, MD. Last year's rank: Number 25 in the world.

#15: 167 votes. Donna McGrath.

TOP 20: ★★★★

#16: 98 votes. Karina Voroshilova (USA).

#17: 77 votes. Allison Hayes. Last year's rank: Number 24 in the world

#18: 75 votes. Melissa Stamps. Last year's rank: Number 76 in the world.

#19: 73 votes. Michelle McKinney.

#20: 71 votes. Tina Saelee (USA/Thailand). Last year's rank: Number 50 in the world.

TOP 25: ★★★★

#21: 20 votes. Dina Vitantonio.

#22: 16 votes. David Beck.

#23: 16 votes. Jerry Yusko.

#24: 7 votes. Lorie Johnson.

Honorable Mention:

Amy Cavanaugh
Angela Bixby
Brenda Tenerelli
Caryn Jacobson
Celia M. Caulfield
Charles Lightwalker
Cheryl Johnson
Chris Duphrene
Christine Corda
Colette Baron Reid
Elisa Medhus, Dr.
Gabriela Castillo
Georgia Marantos, MD
Hillary Freitas
Jamie Butler
Janet Bowerman
Jean Sulch

Jennifer Farley
Jethro Smith
Jill Battista
Kelly Coulter
Lee Papa
Misty Sevy
Oktobre Taylor
Renee Alexander
Sandy Helms
Saundra Greene
Steven Farmer, Dr.
Stevie Vnuk
Teresa L. Powers
Terri Daniel
Trilby Johnson

*** *** ***

PHOTOS' GALLERY OF THE LAST YEAR'S BEST HEALERS IN THE UNITED STATES

Strangely enough, some very distinguished healers in this section and who scored highly in the previous vote, did not make it this year!! Nevertheless, I am herewith including them for the record, along the votes they received last year and their world's rank.

2012 World Rank: Dean Kraft (USA) (3rd Place)

*** *** ***

2012 World Rank: Jack Gray (USA) (4th Place)

2012 World Rank: Roger Laborde (USA) (5th Place)

2012 World Rank: Dr. Issam Nemeh, MD (USA) (16th Place)

2012 World Rank: Barbara Brennan (USA) (19th Place)

2012 World Rank: Dr. Steven Weiss, MD (USA) (20th Place)

2012 World Rank: Rosalyn Bruyere, DD (USA) (21st Place)

2012 World Rank: Dr. Dolores Krieger, RN, Ph.D. (USA)
(22nd Place)

2012 World Rank: Carolyn Myss (USA) (22nd Place)

2012 World Rank: Johanna Morgan, MA, CHT (USA) (23rd Place)

2012 World Rank: Allison Hayes (USA) (24th Place in the world)

2012 World Rank: Carolyn B. Coleridge, MSW, LCSW (USA) (24th Place)

2012 World Rank: Dr. Benjamin Spock, MD (USA) (25th Place)

2012 World Rank: Martha Piesco Hoff (USA) (25th Place)

2012 World Rank: Tiffany Bil (USA) (29th Place)

2012 World Rank: Marla Phillips (USA) (30th Place)

2012 World Rank: Alicia Mary Smith (USA) (30th Place)

2012 World Rank: Tina Saelee (Thailand/USA) (30th Place)

2012 World Rank: Trijntje Reilly (USA) (31st Place)

BEST REIKI PRACTITIONERS IN THE UNITED STATES
By alphabetical order.

A
- Alana Foy (USA)
- Antoinette Hemmerich (USA)

B
- Bonnie Buddin (USA)

C
- Caroline Musial (USA)
- Colleen Benelli (USA)
- Crista Sokolow (USA)

D
- Debra Davies (USA)
- Doreen (DC) Love (USA)

E
- Eileen Boettcher (USA)
- Emery Lauten (USA)

F
- Faye Drummond (USA)

H
- Harriet Shager (USA)

J
- Judy Kelly (USA)

K

- Khatie Lipinski (USA)

L

  Linda Messerman (USA)
- Lynn Boggess (USA)

M

- Mary Ellen Foster (USA)
- Melissa Adams (USA)
- Michelle Sheahan (USA)

N

- Nida Davis (USA)

P

- Patricia Naffki (USA)
- Patricia Williams (USA)
- Peg Jones (USA)

R

- Roger Nobles (USA) Non-traditional/At distance
- Ruth Larkin (USA)

S

- Sallie Bruno (USA)
- Sandra Trimble (USA)
- Sandy Priester (USA)
- Susannah Spanton (USA)
- Suzanne Rollof (USA)

T

- Teresa Rudd (USA)

- Tereza Jantz (USA)

W
- Willian Rand (USA)

By national rank order.

TOP 5 REIKI PRACTITIONERS IN THE US :
★★★★★
In 1st Place:
- Ruth Larkin
In 2nd Place:
- William Rand
In 3rd Place:

Ruth Larkin (USA).

Roger Nobles. William Rand.

Roger Nobles (Non-Traditional/At distance)
- **In 4ᵗʰ Place:**
- Susannah Spanton
- **In 5ᵗʰ Place:**
- Faye Drummond

TOP 10 REIKI PRACTITIONERS IN US :
- **In 6ᵗʰ Place:**
- Judy Kelly
- **In 7ᵗʰ Place:**
- Antoinette Hemmerich
- **In 8ᵗʰ Place:**
- Patricia Naffki
- **In 9ᵗʰ Place:**
- Michelle Sheahan
- **In 10ᵗʰ Place:**
- Lynn Boggess

TOP 15 REIKI PRACTITIONERS IN US :
- **In 11ᵗʰ Place:**
- Caroline Musial
- **In 12ᵗʰ Place:**
- Debra Davies
- **In 13ᵗʰ Place:**
- Khatie Lipinski
- **In 14ᵗʰ Place:**
- Tereza Jantz
- **In 15ᵗʰ Place:**
- Alana Foy

TOP 20 REIKI PRACTITIONERS IN THE US :

- **In 16ᵗʰ Place:**
- Linda Messerman
- **In 17ᵗʰ Place:**
- Harriet Shager

- **In 18th Place:**
- Bonnie Buddin
- **In 19th Place:**
- Sandra Trimble
- **In 20th Place:**
- Patricia Williams
- **In 19th Place:**
- Mary Ellen Foster (USA)
- **In 20th Place:**
- Emery Lauten (USA)

TOP 25 REIKI PRACTITIONERS IN THE US:

- **In 21st Place:**
- Sallie Bruno
- **In 22nd Place:**
- Teresa Rudd
- **In 23rd Place:**
- Suzanne Rollof
- **In 24th Place:**
- Colleen Benelli
- **In 25th Place:**
- Melissa Adams

TOP 30 REIKI PRACTITIONERS IN THE US:

- **In 26th Place:**
- Sandy Priester
- **In 27th Place:**
- Nida Davis
- **In 28th Place:**
- Crista Sokolow
- **In 29th Place:**
- Doreen (DC) Love
- **In 30th Place:**
- Eileen Boettcher

Others:

- **In 31st Place:**
- Peg Jones

BEST PET REIKI PRACTITIONERS IN THE UNITED STATES

In alphabetical order:
- Christine Barnett
- Diane Anderson
- Jean Brusavich
- Joanne Belle
- Kathleen Prasad
- Linda Messerman
- Sarah Hauser
- Sheryl Berger

By national rank order.

Top 5 Pet Reiki (Animal Reiki) in the US:
- **In 1st place:**
- Linda Messerman
- **In 2nd place:**
- Christine Barnett
- **In 3rd place:**
- Kathleen Prasad
- **In 4th place:**
- Jean Brusavich
- **In 5th place**
- Joanne Belle

Linda Messerman. Christine Barnett.

Kathleen Prasad. Jean Brusavich.

Top 10 Pet Reiki (Animal Reiki) in the US: ★★★★★
- **In 6th place**
- Diane Anderson
- **In 7th place**
- Sarah Hauser
- **In 8th place**
- Sheryl Berger

Diane Anderson. Sarah Hauser.

BEST CRYSTAL AND STONE ENERGY AND HEALING PRACTITIONERS IN THE UNITED STATES

By alphabetical order.

- · Allison Hayes
- · Chanda Reaves
- · Dina Vitantonio
- · Lorie Johnson
- · Mary Ellen Collins
- · Roger Nobles

By national rank Order.

Top 5: ★★★★★

- · **In 1st Place:**
- · Allison Hayes
- · **In 2nd Place:**
- · Dina Vitantonio
- · **In 3rd Place:**
- · Lorie Johnson
- · **In 4th Place:**
- · Mary Ellen Collins
- · **In 5th Place:**
- · Mary Ellen Collins

Top 10: ★★★★

- · **In 6th Place:**
- · Chanda Reaves
- · **In 7th Place:**
- · Mary Ellen Collins
- · **In 8th Place:**
- · Roger Nobles

BEST ASTROLOGERS IN THE UNITED STATES

By alphabetical order.

B

- Bob Marks

C

- Clarissa Bernhardt

D

- Daniel Dowd
- David Lawrence Palmer
- Deb McBride
- Debra Clement
- Dennis Flaherty

E

- Eric Linter

F

- Faith McInerney

I

- Iris Saltzman

J

- Jamie Baucco
- Janice King
- Jessica Lanyadoo

L

- Linda Black
- Loretta Standley, Dr.

M

- Michael Lutin

P

- Patrice Cole
- Patricia Norris

R

- Rick Borutta

S

- Sandra Helton
- Sharita Star

T

- Terry Nazon

V

- Virginia Bell
- Vivian Carol

*** *** ***

By national Rank Order. 4 and 5 Stars:

TOP 5 ASTROLOGERS IN THE US : ★★★★★
- **In 1st Place:**
- Patrice Cole
- **In 2nd Place:**
- Debra Clement
- Eric Linter
- **In 3rd Place:**
- Iris Saltzman
- Terry Nazon
- **In 4th Place:**
- Jessica Lanyadoo
- Rick Borutta

Patrice Cole (USA).

Debra Clement. Eric Linter.

- **In 5th Place:**
- Iris Saltzman
- Terry Nazon

TOP 10 ASTROLOGERS IN THE US :

- **In 6th Place:**
- Jessica Lanyadoo
- Rick Borutta

Rick Borutta (USA)
Photo Credit Robert Schulze

- **In 7th Place:**
- Michael Lutin
- **In 8th Place:**
- Deb McBride
- **In 9th Place:**
- Vivian Carol
- **In 10th Place:**
- Faith McInerney

TOP 15 ASTROLOGERS IN THE US :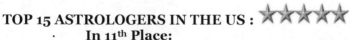
- **In 11th Place:**
- Karen Thorne
- **In 12th Place:**
- Daniel Dowd
- **In 13th Place:**
- Linda Black
- **In 14th Place:**
- Virginia Bell
- **In 15th Place:**
- Clarissa Bernhardt.
- Loretta Standley, Dr.

TOP 20 ASTROLOGERS IN THE US : ★★★★★
- **In 16th Place:**
- Sandra Helton.
- **In 17th Place:**
- Bob Marks
- **In 18th Place:**
- David Lawrence Palmer
- **In 19th Place:**
- Dennis Flaherty
- **In 20th Place:**
- Jamie Baucco

TOP 25 ASTROLOGERS IN THE US : ★★★★
- **In 21st Place:**
- Janice King
- **In 22nd Place:**
- Patricia Norris
- **In 23rd Place:**
- Sharita Star

***   ***   ***

BEST NUMEROLOGISTS IN THE UNITED STATES

TOP 5 NUMEROLOGISTS IN US : ★★★★★
- In 1st **Place:**
- Patrice Cole
- In 2nd **Place:**
- Glynis McCants
- In 3rd **Place:**
- Maria Shaw-Lawson
- In 4th **Place:**
- Name removed (USA)
- In 5th **Place:**
- Nicolas David Ngan (USA)

*** *** ***

BEST WITCH (WHITE MAGICK) IN THE UNITED STATES

Patti Negri : ★★★★★

185

BEST PET PSYCHICS/ANIMAL COMMUNICATORS IN THE UNITED STATES

By alphabetical order.

A

- Annette Betche

B

- Barbara DeLong
- Barbara Morrison
- Barbara Rawson
- Bill Northern

C

- Carol Gurney
- Catherine Fergusson
- Christina Nelson

D

- DC Love

J

- Jeannie Lindheim
- Jennifer Wallens
- Jeri Ryan
- Jethro Smith
- Joan Ranquet

K

- Karen Wrigley
- Kristin Thompson

L

- Lorraine Turner
- Lydia Hiby
- Linda Messerman
- Lorie Johnson

M

- Mandy Carr
- Margo Russell (France/USA)
- Martha Williams
- Mary Marshall
- Maureen Harmonay
- Melissa Bacelar

P

- Pam Case
- Patricia Richards
- Penelope Smith

R

- Rachel Marie
- Rae Ramsey

S

- Samantha Hall
- Sharon Warner
- Sindi Somers
- Solana
- Sonya Fitzpatrick
- Stan Kestral
- Steven D. Farmer, MD
- Sue Hopple
- Sue Manley
- Sue Pike

- Susan Deren

By national Rank Order.
TOP 5 PET PSYCHICS & ANIMAL COMMUNICATORS
IN THE US : ★★★★★
- **In 1st Place:**
- Joan Ranquet
- Jennifer Wallens
- **In 2nd Place:**
- Carol Gurney
- **In 3rd Place:**
- Lydia Hiby
- **In 4th Place:**
- Penelope Smith
- **In 5th Place:**
- Martha Williams

Joan Ranquet. Jennifer Wallens.

Carol Gurney.Lydia Hiby. Penelope Smith

TOP 10 PET PSYCHICS & ANIMAL COMMUNICATORS
IN THE US : ★★★★★

- **In 6th Place**
- Mandy Carr
- Linda Messerman

Martha Williams. Linda Messerman

- **In 7th Place:**
- Sonya Fitzpatrick
- **In 8th Place:**
- Barbara Rawson
- **In 9th Place:**
- Karen Wrigley
- **In 10th Place:**
- Pam Case

TOP 15 PET PSYCHICS & ANIMAL COMMUNICATORS
IN THE US : ★★★★★

- **In 11th Place:**
- Jeri Ryan (USA)
- **In 12th Place:**

- Kristin Thompson ★★★★
- **In 13th Place:**
- Sue Pike
- **In 14th Place:**
- Mary Marshall

190

- In 15th **Place:**
- Bill Northern

TOP 20 PET PSYCHICS & ANIMAL COMMUNICATORS IN THE US :
- In 16th **Place:**
- Susan Deren
- In 17th **Place:**
- Sue Hopple (USA)
- In 18th **Place:**
- Catherine Fergusson (USA)
- In 19th **Place:**
- Maureen Harmonay (USA)
- In 20th **Place:**
- Jeannie Lindheim (USA)

TOP 25 PET PSYCHICS & ANIMAL COMMUNICATORS IN THEUS: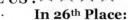
- In 21st **Place:**
- Annette Betcher
- In 22nd **Place:**
- Barbara Morrison
- In 23rd **Place:**
- Sharon Warner
- In 24th **Place:**
- Melissa Bacelar
- In 25th **Place:**
- Sindi Somers
- Steven D. Farmer, MD

TOP 30 PET PSYCHICS & ANIMAL COMMUNICATORS IN THE US :
- In 26th **Place:**
- Rae Ramsey
- In 27th **Place:**
- Sue Manley

- **In 28th Place:**
- Jethro Smith
- **In 29th Place:**
- Barbara DeLong
- **In 30th Place:**
- Christina Nelson

TOP 35 PET PSYCHICS & ANIMAL COMMUNICATORS IN THE US : ★★★★

- **In 31st Place:**
- DC Love
- **In 32nd Place:**
- Lorraine Turner
- **In 33rd Place:**
- Patricia Richards
- **In 34th Place:**
- Rachel Marie
- **In 35th Place:**
- Samantha Hall

TOP 40 PET PSYCHICS & ANIMAL COMMUNICATORS IN THE US : ★★★★

- **In 36th Place:**
- Solana
- **In 37th Place:**
- Stan Kestral
- **In 38th Place:**
- Lorie Johnson

*** *** ***

BEST PALMISTS IN THE UNITED STATES

By national Rank Order.

TOP 5 PALMISTS IN THE WORLD : ★★★★★
- **In 1st Place:**
- Mark Seltman (USA)
- **In 2nd Place:**
- Joe Nicols
- **In 3rd Place:**
- Edward Shanahan

*** *** ***

BEST FENG SHUI PRACTITIONERS IN THE UNITED STATES

By alphabetical order.

A

- Alexandra Shaw
- Anita Rosenberg

D

- Dawn Champine
- Diane Hiller

L

- Larry Sang

M

- Master Yau
- Melissa Stamps

P

- Pun Yin (China-USA)

By national rank order.

TOP 5 FENG SHUI MASTERS/PRACTITIONERS IN THE US :
- **In 1st Place:** ★★★★★
- Anita Rosenberg
- **In 2nd Place:**
- Diane Hiller
- **In 3rd Place:**

- Pun Yin (China-USA/Chine-USA)
- **In 4ᵗʰ Place:**
- Larry Sang

Anita Rosenberg (USA)   Diane Hiller (USA).

- **In 5ᵗʰ Place:**
- Master Yau (USA)

TOP 10 FENG SHUI MASTERS/PRACTITIONERS IN THE US :

- **In 6ᵗʰ Place:**
- Melissa Stamps
- **In 7ᵗʰ Place:**
- Dawn Champine
- **In 8ᵗʰ Place**
- Alexandra Shaw

*** *** ***

BEST SPIRIT ARTISTS IN THE UNITED STATES

By alphabetical order.

A

- Anny Rose Newman
- Abby Rose

C

- Coral Ryder
- Courtney Kimmick

G

- Ginny Ciszek

J

- Janette Kaye
- Janette Oakman
- Jennifer Wallens
- Joseph Shiel
- Joyce Markwick

L

- Lisa Nevot
- Lori Marshall
- Lorraine Turner

M

- Mark Sanders
- Michael and Marti Parry

R

- Rita Berkowitz
- Rosalind Coleman

S

- Sue Reeder (USA)

By national order. 5 and 4 Stars:

TOP 5 SPIRIT ARTISTS IN THE US : ★★★★★

- **In 1ˢᵗ Place:**
- Jennifer Wallens
- **In 2ⁿᵈ Place:**
- Janette Kaye
- **In 3ʳᵈ Place:**
- Rosalind Coleman
- **In 4ᵗʰ Place:**
- Rita Berkowitz
- Lisa Nevot
- **In 5ᵗʰ Place:**
- Lori Marshall

Jennifer Wallens.

Janette Kaye. .Rosalind Coleman.

Lisa Nevot. Rita Berkowitz.

TOP 10 SPIRIT ARTISTS IN THE US : ★★★★★
- **In 6ᵗʰ Place:**

Lori Marshall (USA)

- **In 7ᵗʰ Place:**
- Joyce Markwick
- **In 8ᵗʰ Place:**
- Joseph Shiel
- **In 9ᵗʰ Place:**
- Ginny Ciszek
- **In 10th Place:**
- Mark Sanders

TOP 15 SPIRIT ARTISTS IN THE US : ★★★★
- **In 11ᵗʰ Place:**
- Sue Reeder
- **In 12ᵗʰ Place:**
- Michael and Marti Parry
- **In 13ᵗʰ Place:**
- Coral Ryder

- **In 14th Place:**
- Janette Oakman (USA)
- **In 15th Place:**
- Lorraine Turner

TOP 20 SPIRIT ARTISTS IN THE US : ★★★★
- **In 16th Place:**
- Anny Rose Newman
- **In 17th Place:**
- Abby Rose (USA)
- **In 18th Place:**
- Susan Averre (USA)
- **In 19th Place:**
- Susan Averre (USA)
- Joseph Shiel (USA)

*** *** ***

BEST PSYCHIC DETECTIVES IN THE UNITED STATES
(Crimes and Missing Persons)

By national rank order.

Top 5:

- **In 1st Place:**
- Phil Jordan ★★★★★
- **In 2nd Place:**
- Shellee Halle ★★★★★
- **In 3rd Place:**
- Noreen Renier: ★★★
- **In 4th Place:**
- Chuck Bergman: ★★★
- **In 5th Place:**
- Dawn "Mystic Haven" Mitchell: ★★

In 6th Place:

- Jan Drake-Bakke: ★★

*** *** ***

BEST DREAM INTERPRETERS IN THE UNITED STATES

By alphabetical order.
- Ann Cutler, MA
- Brenton Harris
- Craig Webb
- Damian Nordmann
- Darlene Lancer, JD
- Jane Teresa Anderson
- John Seed Bearer
- Kristopher Kotch
- Lauri Quinn Loewenberg
- Leila Esber
- Linda Shandr
- Mary Ann Kotch
- Maxson J. McDowell PhD, LMSW, LP
- Nancy Wagaman, MA
- Roger Nobles
- Ross J. Miller
- Tarah Harper

By national rank order. 5 and 4 stars:

TOP 5 DREAM INTERPRETERS IN THE US : ★★★★★
- **In 1st Place :**
- Lauri Quinn Loewenberg
- **In 2nd Place :**
- Jane Teresa Anderson
- **In 3rd Place :**
- Darlene Lancer, JD
- Tarah Harper
- **In 4th Place :**
- Craig Webb
- **In 5th Place :**
- Kristopher Kotch
- Mary Ann Kotch

Lauri Quinn Loewenberg

Jane Teresa Anderson. Darlene Lancer, JD

Tarah Harper

TOP 10 DREAM INTERPRETERS IN THE US : ★★★★
- **In 6th Place :**
- Ann Cutler, MA
- **In 7th Place :**

- Nancy Wagaman, MA
- **In 8th Place :**
- Linda Shandra
- **In 9th Place :**
- John Seed Bearer
- **In 10th Place :**
- Ross J. Miller USA)

TOP 15 DREAM INTERPRETERS IN THE US :

- **In 11th Place :**
- Leila Esber
- **In 12th Place :**
- Brenton Harris
- **In 13th Place :**
- Damian Nordmann
- **In 14th Place :**
- Roger Nobles

*** *** ***

BEST SPIRIT PHOTOGRAPHERS-SCRYING MEDIUMS IN THE UNITED STATES

By national rank order: 5 and 4 stars:
In 1st place:

Tara Viosca Mead (
In 2nd place:

Robyne Marie, Reverend ★★★★★
In 3rd place:

Sherie Hurd Roufusse (Canada/USA) ★★★★

Tara Viosca Mead (USA).

Robyne Marie. Sherie Hurd Roufusse

*** *** ***

BEST LIFE COACHES-PSYCHICS IN THE UNITED STATES

In alphabetical order:

A

    Angela Bixby, Reverend

C

    Corbie Mitleid, Reverend

D

    Daved Beck
    Diane Hiller
    Doyle Ward

K

    Kimberly Ward, Reverend

L

    Linda Carney

M

    Melissa Berman
    Melissa Stamps

P

    Pamela Beaty, Reverend
    PennyC.

S

    Shannon Leischner
    Suzanne Grace

In national rank order. 5 and 4 stars:

TOP 5 LIFE COACHES-PSYCHICS IN THE US: ★★★★★

- **In 1st Place :**
- Suzanne Grace
- **In 2nd Place :**
- Melissa Berman
- **In 3rd Place:**
- Diane Hiller
- **In 4th Place:**
- Melissa Stamps
- **In 5th Place:**
  Kimberly Ward, Reverend

Suzanne Grace (USA). Melissa Berman (USA).

Diane Hiller (USA). Melissan Stamps (USA).

Kimberly Ward (USA).

TOP 10 LIFE COACHES-PSYCHICS IN THE US: ★★★★★

- **In 6th Place:**
- Pamela Beaty, Reverend
- **In 7th Place:**
- Corbie Mitleid, Reverend
- **In 8th Place:**
- Doyle Ward
- **In 9th Place:**
- Angela Bixby, Reverend
- **In 10th Place:**
- Shannon Leischner

Pamela Beaty. Corbie Mitleid.

Doyle Ward. Angela Bixby.

Shannon Leischner.

TOP 15 LIFE COACHES-PSYCHICS IN THE US: ★★★★★
- **In 11th Place:**
- PennyC.
- **In 12th Place:**
- Linda Carney
- David Beck

***   ***   ***

212

PennyC (USA). Linda Carney (USA).

David Beck (USA).

BEST PARANORMAL RESEARCHERS/INVESTIGATORS IN THE UNITED STATES

Note: This includes lightworkers on site (In the field).

By alphabetical order.

- Bj Haggerty
- Clyde Lewis
- Dave Schrader
- Dave Young
- George Noory
- Grant Wilson
- Jennifer Wallens
- Jethro Smith
- Kim Russo
- Leslie Shapiro
- Lyle Sharman
- Patti Negri
- Ray Schmidt
- Samantha Hawes
- Steve Blaze

By national rank order.

TOP 5 : ★★★★★

- **In 1st Place:**
- George Noory
- **In 2nd Place:**
- Clyde Lewis
- **In 3rd Place:**
- Jennifer Wallens
- **In 4th Place:**
- Kim Russo
- **In 5th Place:**
- Jethro Smith
- Patti Negri

TOP 10: ★★★★

- **In 6th Place:**
- Steve Blaze
- Dave Young
- **In 7th Place:**
- Ray Schmidt
- **In 8th Place:**
- Grant Wilson
- **In 9th Place:**
- Dave Schrader
- **In 10th Place:**
- Leslie Shapiro

TOP 15: ★★★★

- **In 11th Place:**
- Leslie Shapiro (
- Samantha Hawes
- **In 12th Place:**
- Lyle Sharman
- **In 13th Place:**
- Bj Haggerty

*** *** ***

BEST GHOST HUNTERS/PERSONALITIES IN THE UNITED STATES

By alphabetical order. : ★★★★★
- Bj Haggerty
- Dave Young
- Grant Wilson
- Leslie Shapiro
- Samanta Hawes
- Steve Blaze

Dave Young .Grant Wilson.

Samanta Hawes. Steve Blaze.

Dave Young

BEST PARANORMAL RADIO SHOW HOSTS IN THE UNITED STATES

By alphabetical order.
- Amy Cavanaugh
- Barbara DeLong
- Belle Salisbury
- Chris from Curious Times
- Clyde Lewis
- Dave Schrader
- George Noory
- Janine Regan Sinclair
- Jethro Smith
- Kelly Coulter
- Linda Irwin
- Pamela Cummins
- Patti Negri
- Renee Richards
- Saundra Greene
- Solana

By national Rank Order. ★★★★★
- **In 1st Place:**
- George Noory
- **In 2nd Place:**
- Clyde Lewis
- **In 3rd Place:**
- Jethro Smith
- **In 4th Place:**
- Patti Negri
- **In 5th Place:**

- Dave Schrader: ★★★★

- **In 6th Place:** ★★★
- Amy Cavanaugh
- Barbara DeLong
- **In 7th Place:**
- Belle Salisbury

- **In 8th Place:** ⭐⭐⭐
- Chris from Curious Times
- Janine Regan Sinclair

- **In 9th Place:** ⭐⭐⭐
- Kelly Coulter
- Linda Irwin
- Pamela Cummins

- **In 10th Place:** ⭐⭐⭐
- Renee Richards
- Saundra Greene
- Solana

*** *** ***

BEST PARANORMAL TV SHOWS IN THE UNITED STATES

Category by alphabetical order.

- Ghost Adventures ★★★★★
- Ghost Hunters ★★★★★
- Haunted ★★★★★
- Reincarnated-Past Lives ★★★★
- The Ghost Inside My Child ★★★★
- The Haunting of ★★★★

*** *** ***

BEST INTUITIVE ENTERTAINERS IN THE US.

By alphabetical order.

- Jethro Smith (USA): ★★★★
- Patrice Cole (USA): ★★★★★
- Patti Negri: (USA): ★★★★★

*** *** ***

PROFILES AND INTERVIEWS WITH SOME OF THE BEST LIGHTWORKERS IN THE UNITED STATES.

Suzanne Grace

Brief bio and personal statement by Suzanne Grace: I am a full time psychic medium and life coach but am also a CASA Advocate for children (Court Appointed Special Advocate) whereby I represent the interests of children in foster care in the court system to ensure that they have a voice. As children are a passion of mine, I also work with those with gifts in my free time in order to ensure they can grow into their gifts feeling confident instead of fearful. I am a wife and mother to four amazing souls who are the best part of me and who all inspire me to be the best person I can be. I live just outside of Los Angeles, CA, but I have clients worldwide. I am entering my 16th year of business and I find that I grow daily - my clients teach me more than I could have ever imagined.

I have been tested and certified by the American Federation of Psychics, Mediums and Healers; I have also been tested and certified by James van Praagh, Charles Virtue, ESPsychics.com as well as Bob Olson's Best Psychic Directory. I can be most easily reached via my website www.suzannegracemedium.com or via email
sgracemedium@gmail.com

Question: What is the most important revelation or message you have received from the world of spirit? And in your opinion, where is located the world of spirit. And what the souls of dead people and other spirits do in the after life?

Suzanne Grace: The world of spirit resides just on the other side of the veil.

Answer: The most important message I have received from spirit is to love unconditionally; whether our beliefs center around God, Buddha, etc, does not matter as the message is all the same - to love one another, to share and show that love to one another.

The world of spirit resides just on the other side of the veil; it is a dimension next to ours, one we can easily see if we choose to be open to doing so.

What I have seen on the other side is that each soul has their own individual definition of heaven; if heaven is fishing on the open seas that is where you will find that particular soul. If heaven is

224

being surrounded by beautiful gardens, that is where you will find that soul. Heaven is our heaven but so much more than what we mere humans can understand.

Question: How would/could you help your clients?
Via guidance? Spiritual comfort?
Giving them messages from the world beyond? Foreseeing their future? Or......?
Answer: I help my clients by giving them practical information infused with that which their guides, angels and loved ones would like for them to hear; as each clients needs are individual in nature, I tend to listen to what their guides, loved ones and angels would like for them to know and then address any specific questions the client may have. As I channel each message, I tend to recall very little of what has been said but I do know that my clients have told me that not only are my readings infused with love and wisdom, but also with personal messages designed just for them.
I do not deliver a generic message as each person has individual needs. I have delivered information on the future but I find that this should be limited as each person much live and experience in order to grow and that is not for me to do for them; in some cases, they do need to guidance on how to get there and that is part of the spiritual counseling and life coaching I offer.

Question: What evidence do you have on the survival of the human soul? Are you able to contact the soul of dead people? If so, how do you do it? What is your technique?

Suzanne Grace: I simply ask my guides to bring forward the loved ones with the most urgent messages.

Answer:
I have been speaking with the passed over human soul since I was a child. I love working with and channeling messages from departed loved ones as it brings peace and closure to many. In most cases, I simply ask my guides to bring forward the loved ones with the most urgent messages. In terms of technique, I am not really sure how others do it, but I know for me, I simply ask

225

for the loved one to present me with information that could not otherwise be known as validation for the client.

Once the client feels that they are indeed working with their loved one, I then channel the messages and as I mentioned before, I tend to not have any recollection of the conversation, although I am wholly present during the reading.

In some cases, if a client is fearful of the message, I will hold their hand, reassure them they have nothing to fear and create a loving and safe environment in which they are free to allow their emotions to surface.

There is no judgment and I have learned that it is not up to me to judge the message, simply deliver it.

However, I am adamant about a few things: I will not discuss death dates as this is NOT my job and it is not one I feel should be discussed as we all have free will to make changes. I will not deliver information that I am unsure of as well; if spirit is being vague, the message is not meant to be known.

I have witnessed too many who do not realize that they are holding another's wellbeing in their hands and they deliver life altering messages haphazardly and this is not fair to the client. If you are unsure, do not speak it, do not deliver it as what you say can negatively impact another's life and that is not our role as mediums.

Info Box:
Contact: sgracemedium@gmail.com or
www.suzannegracemedium.com or ESPsychics.com
Best time to contact you: anytime!
Do you accept clients from foreign countries? Yes, absolutely.
What are your fees and rates in general?
How much do you charge?
Because I work for ESPsychics.com as well as my own private clients and do not want to compete against myself, I offer the same rates that ESPsychics.com does.
We have a tiered program, 5 minutes on up - and while this is equal to $240 per hour, we are also negotiable at times. We want to ensure that those who need us can afford to work with us. We also offer group rates which vary by the number of people in attendance.

Roger Nobles

Brief bio and personal statement by Roger Nobles: My name is Roger Nobles, I'm divorced, 1 daughter and 3 grandchildren, 2 boys and 1 girl. Born in Alabama, now live in Leander, Texas, USA. I retired from the U.S. Air Force following a 24 year career.

My formal education includes 2 Associate degrees, one in computer science, and the other in print journalism with additional undergraduate classes in Psychology, Sociology, along with Communication as a theoretical science. I'm a member of "The International Reiki and Energy Healers Guild."
Also I'm a Master Teacher for Usui Reiki Ryoho, Karuna Ki Reiki, Ascension Reiki, and an Ordained Minister with the Universal Life Church ULC where I was also been awarded a Doctor of Divinity degree. Additionally, I've completed several courses in Color and Crystal therapy; I hope to become certified in both disciplines very soon.

Question: What is the most important revelation or message you have received from the world of spirit?
And in your opinion, where is located the world of spirit. And what the souls of dead people and other spirits do in the after life?

Roger Nobles: I don't believe in an end world.

Answer: The most important message I've received from spirit is the lesson of Butterfly – "Death is not to be feared for the grave is like a cocoon – a temporary place of growth and change, opening into a beautiful new world."
I don't believe in an end world – We develop and grow in this physical plane and when our journey is completed, we merge into a state of "oneness," finished along with all members of our Soul Family – "Oneness" steps forward onto a new journey and continues to develop and grow until it also reaches the next plane of being – the journey is without end, simple stops along the way to put on a new set of "clothes" or form.
I call the place Summerland where we temporarily stay reviewing accomplishments and lessons learned during past incarnations and prepare for the next phase of our journey until the rest of our soul family arrives.

Question: How would/could you help your clients?
Via guidance? Spiritual comfort? Giving them messages from the world beyond? Foreseeing their future? Or......?

Answer: I teach Usui Reiki in two courses, one is a Practitioner program Level 1 -Level 3 Master Practitioner and the other is Level 4 Master Teacher program.
I also teach Spiritual Development and am a Life Coach.
I've written Training Manuals for all 3 classes.

Question: What evidence do you have on the survival of the human soul? Are you able to contact the soul of dead people? If so, how do you do it? What is your technique?

Roger Nobles: I often have conversations with Spirit, not only of this dimension but of many.

Answer: Evidence of spirit is not of the physical but of faith and belief. After my father died, he sat at the end of my bed and talked with me, gave messages to pass to the rest of our family. When my mother passed some 25 years later, I saw him standing above her coffin. I saw her rise to meet him, hand in hand they turn and looked at me and with a big smile and a wave from both, they turned again to walk away, still holding hands, and I saw them enter the land of mists. I often have conversations with Spirit, not only of this dimension but of many. No guides, No demands or commands, we are friends; my Lady of the Mysts is my best friend and mentor.

Info Box:
I may be contacted: via email: alabeanz@yahoo.com
Facebook: https://www.facebook.com/roger.nobles.39
Phone: 1-512-635-0649. Best time to contact me is anytime
 Do you accept clients from foreign countries? Yes
 What is your website?
Facebook groups - 1.Main Group for Spiritual Development – Mystic Development
https://www.facebook.com/groups/220405848114047/
 2. Reiki Practitioners - Mystic's Free Usui Reiki Training and Healing Circle
https://www.facebook.com/groups/1430346247233598/

3. Reiki Teachers - Mystic's Usui Reiki Master Teacher Free Training Program
https://www.facebook.com/groups/545077428951329/

4. Free Healing Group (also offers Usui Reiki Level III Master Practitioner Training) – We are One –
https://www.facebook.com/groups/146428208859679/
5.Delicate, Emotional, sensitive issues, including grief counseling - Mystic Circle
https://www.facebook.com/groups/1425925140953700/
6. For Advertising and Promotions - Mystic's Trading Post - for all your Spiritual needs –
https://www.facebook.com/groups/652334308218998/
What are your fees and rates in general? How much do you charge?
Seriously – a smile and a commitment to help others – Donations will be accepted but are not necessary. Visit and like my Facebook Page for Inspirational Stories, Quotes, Songs Graphics - Inspirational Journey
https://www.facebook.com/CrowsJourney

*** *** ***

Dianne Hiller

Diane Hiller is a Psychic Medium, Medical Intuitive, Psychotherapist and Certified Feng Shui Master.
She is an innovative expert in the field of metaphysics.
She is a former nurse and phi beta kappa receiving both her undergraduate degree in Psychology and Master's in Clinical Social Work at The University of Connecticut. Diane has extensively studied both Buddhism and Shamanism and received certification as a Black Sect Tibetan Buddhist Feng Shui Master TM.

This professional training program was originally formed at the request and under the guidance the late His Holiness Professor Thomas Lin Yun, a world-renowned expert in Feng Shui. She is a member in good standing with The International Feng Shui Guild.
Diane's psychic gifts were evident at the age of nine. They fully awakened during her personal healing journey, through the study of shamanism and chakra journeywork, and following two very powerful kundalini openings. She is founder and owner of Elemental Empowerments, LLC, in Litchfield, Connecticut and combines the arts of Mediumship, Psychotherapy, Feng Shui, and spiritual life coaching in her professional practice.
Diane's educational background and skills give her insight and understanding of your life challenges and her spiritual toolbox is full of abilities to work with you on numerous energetic levels. It is an honor and privilege for Diane to be of service to you.

Specialty
Psychic Medium, Medical Intuitive, Certified BTB Feng Shui Master TM, Licensed Psychotherapist. Diane reads locally in her Litchfield office and does phone readings both in the USA and Internationally.
Fees: Mediumship $195 60 min, $165 45 min (group and couple rates are also available). Psychic readings $125 for 30 min $65 for 15 min. Feng Shui- In home $200 hr. (2 hr. minimum) $150 hr. thereafter. Phone floor plan readings are also available

Contact Diane for quotes on Corporate Events, Psychic Parties, Group Events and Classes. Please see website for other offerings.
Payment accepted via Pay Pal or Credit Card via The Square
Contact information
Phone-860-601-1263
Email- dianehiller@optonline.net

Website: Elementalempowerments.com
Facebook:
https://www.facebook.com/DianeHillerPsychicMedium?ref=hl
Skype: DianeHiller99

Education

Bachelor of Arts in Psychology (summa cum laude, phi beta kappa)
Master's in Social Work, Major in Clinical, Minor in Research
Former LPN and Real Estate Agent

Awards

Phi Beta Kappa Society
Named in the 2014 edition of "The Top 100 Psychics and Astrologers in America" by Paulette Cooper and Paul Noble.
Featured as one of 26 Top Mediums Worldwide in the first Ever "World Visionary Summit" in 2012 By Spiritual Living.com

*** *** ***

Patti Negri (first from left) on stage.

Patti Negri

Brief bio and personal statement by Patti Negri, the first lady of the occult: I am a psychic, medium and "good" witch.

I live in Hollywood, California and due to my entertainment background I work a lot in film and television, both on camera and as an expert/consultant. I have both local and International Clientele and over 20 years experience working with one on one with clients, speaking, teaching workshops and also my specialty of house, office and space clearings and my signature séances.

I was voted number one psychic in the US and number one medium, tarot reader and witch/magical practioner in the world for 2013 - 2014.

I am honored to be a Chief Examiner and Sr. Vice President of the American Federation of Certified Psychics and Mediums.

I am grateful to have recently graced several magazine covers including American Psychic & Medium Magazine, Art, UFO and

Supernatural, Parapsychology and Mind Power, Extraterrestrials Magazine and Stars Illustrated and contributing to, or been a part of over 20 books, several of which are Amazon Bestsellers.

Question: What is the most important revelation or message you have received from the world of spirit?
And in your opinion, where is located the world of spirit?
And what the souls of dead people and other spirits do in the afterlife?
Answer: The most important message I have received from spirit truly is that it is all about love.
Hmmm...well, love and intent. Okay, love and intent and action! As the song says – love truly is what makes the world go round – and more importantly, love is what makes it a better place. When we truly come from love – everything we do or say is of a higher vibration.

It is reflected in all our words, actions and therefore results. Intention is important in making things happen.
That "laser beam focus" of intent is what you need to manifest and create the world and the life you want. My belief system and working mode is all based around creating that "laser beam focus" – however you create it --whether you call it magic, spell working, affirmations, prayer, ritual or visualization.
The "action" is what brings it all together.

Patti Negri: Because everyday can be a miracle day if we make it happen!

Yes, I do believe miracles can happen – and do every day – but, I believe god, the creator, source, the universe – whatever words you use - truly does help those who help themselves!
We were given free will.
That free will is the gift that allows us to be the architects of our own life and really create the life we want. But, we need to take the action to make it happen – at least on those "non miracle" days!
Because everyday can be a miracle day if we make it happen!

I believe
that world
of spirit is
everywhere!

In my experience there is no physical space – or even time in that realm. I believe that the souls of dead people do lots of things! One, they become a part of our great ancestral stream. They become a part of the Akashic records, the great consciousness. Two, I think they do watch and look out for their still living loved ones – and communicate if allowed appropriate. Three, I think they continue to learn and grow and move forward in their own evolution – and if evolved or enlightened enough - the evolution of life itself.

Patti Negri: My real goal is to give a clear picture and empower the client.

Question: How would/could you help your clients?
Via guidance? Spiritual comfort? Giving them messages from the world beyond? Foreseeing their future? Or......?
Answer: I help my clients in a variety of ways.
I have no "set pattern". I often start with tarot in a session so I can "tune in" to the person as I read them.
Then, if I see energetic blocks it will often go into a path working, journey or past life session, energy clearing or soul retrieval.
If spirits come in (and are relevant to client) it will sometimes go into mediumship or even communicating with their spirit guides.
Yes, of course I "foresee the future" – but my real goal is to give a clear picture – and then empower the client with tools and information and techniques that will help them when they leave the session as they go back into daily life!

Question: What evidence do you have on the survival of the human soul? Were you able to contact the soul of dead people? If so, how do you do it? What is your technique?
Answer: The evidence of the survival of the human soul has been clear to me my entire life. When I was just a toddler I had real interactions and communications with the souls of dead people. It was just a gift of sight that I was born with. A blessing.
Though, over the years I have developed lots of techniques to communicate with them so that I can include the non-sighted and allow "regular people" to see, feel, communicate and experience these souls as well.
That is where my signature séances, galleries and mediumship have come into being.
Info Box:
Contact:
Ph: 323.461.0640
Email: Patti@PattiNegri.com
Web: www.PattiNegri.com
Twitter: @PattiNegri
FB: https://www.facebook.com/pages/Patti-Negri/540391795983570

Skype: Patti.Negri
-Best time to contact you.
-After 10 AM Pacific Time (or leave a message anytime)
-Do you accept clients from foreign countries?
Yes (I have skype and viber)
-What is your website? www.PattiNegri.com
-What are your fees and rates in general?
-How much do you charge?
-My full sessions are $150.00 for an hour.
That can include readings, mediumship, journey work, spell working or whatever needed. Shorter sessions are available at $113.00 for 45 minutes or $75.00 for 30 minutes for simple, straight readings. (With shorter sessions there is usually not time for journey work, spell working or clearings.

Phone consultation 35 euro and 27 for members of the spiritual world
Personal consultation 80 euro's or 65 euro's for members
My evening thoughts are for free
Every month I give away one free consultation.

*** *** ***

Daved Beck

Brief bio and personal statement by Daved Beck: First I would like to embrace this opportunity to say thank you for co-creating this connection of Unity for all of us. I am a full time Psychic Medium and Life Coach with over 20 years experience connecting and communicating with Spirit.

I presently reside in a suburb of Chicago and work with national and international clients. I am a published author and have been blessed by embracing several opportunities of being interviewed, reviewed and published through several public media outlets (books, magazines, TV and Radio).

I also continue to embrace my passion for dance, choreography and the arts. In 2013, I was honored and blessed to have been nominated and voted by the public to be a recipient of the Lifetime Achievement and inducted into the Lightworker Hall of Fame. I can be reached through www.davedbeck.com and my email Daved@davedbeck.com

Question: What is the most important revelation or message you have received from the world of spirit?

And in your opinion, where is located the world of spirit. And what the souls of dead people and other spirits do in the after life?

Answer: The most important revelation and message I continually receive is love...to love all that is a reflection of our own creation. We are here to expand and be all that we came here to be and that is just in the unity of love that indeed we are. Our loved Ones...Our ancestors, all created of love. They loved us the best way they knew how within their own awareness during their Human experience. They want us to know that whenever we feel alone to know, there is always someone within many by our side.

This love that lingers within the breeze Unique to each One of us, Spirit encourages us to laugh, dance and connect within as much as we can, for we are all the same.

Each of us living in this human existence is nothing less nothing more than love.

When standing within one mind and one heart within just One Intention....to just be love....pain within can and will be healed in the practice to be. Our words and thoughts are the only power of us...nothing to put above or below...What is judged outside of self is that only of how we judge self. Be gentler and kinder within the reflection of self. For the thoughts we speak are the spells we create and what we do put out does come back just not always as exact.

Daved Beck: Everything is connected, everything is energy.

Energy is a continuum, always in constant motion. Within this knowing, it is in my opinion that the World of Soul and Spirit is all around. The Souls and Spirits watch over us and guide us through the signs and message's each unique to our own personal lives. Even we, the Human living, are spirit and soul dancing around...day in day out...continuing to move with our very own beating hearts...Our memories...Our thoughts...Our words spoken....the cells of our being....

Here, there and Everywhere is where the World of Soul and Spirit reside; Guiding us within all that we connect, this is what I

241

believe the after life to be. For eventually we the living here and now will be the unseen dancing within the breeze, moving through the trees in hearts and minds of each our legacy co-creating the Moons and Suns that come to be....Where, When and How is only for One Soul/Spirit/Human within One's own journey to decide. Within all the same and each unique within One.

Question: How would/could you help your clients? Via guidance? Spiritual comfort? Giving them messages from the world beyond? Foreseeing their future? Or......?

Answer: As I state with every client and group I work with in my practice of communicating with Spirit...I will get images, initials, names and sometimes even last names. It is not up for me to judge rather just speak what I get. Sometimes I will say a statement that was once specifically said or a specific date that may mean something...Again it is not for me to judge only to speak what is received....

Sometimes I have been known to speak in other languages that the client is able to understand where to me I thought I was just sounding out the words to formulate the sentence being received. I ask always the recipients to affirm if the information is accurate or if it is not.

I also state that sometimes the information being received may not connect or make sense within that moment of time. They may need to do some research or ask friends or family.

Some information coming through can be an experience being foreseen...in the knowing we all have free will and choice and if we focus on something with enough energy we can indeed create...I do not have that right nor of my personal integrity to say this is how it will come to be for someone's life...this is just something I see and or feel...if in fact it does come to be, please connect with me as so I may honor and congratulate you on the journey. If there is fear within I support the client in embracing and transforming whatever challenge they may be facing into their personal freedom.

Daved Beck: I am a medium between fear and love.

I help uncover the emotional fear that ran through the lineage and support in becoming aware of how emotional fear is showing up in the present in their own lives.

I do encourage if the client wants to ask questions to please do so, for this does support the process in going deeper and understanding. Through the individual or a group session I offer empowering exercises to practice moving forward in their own lives. Sessions with me give from what I have heard and accept to be true, is affirmation, validation, comfort, fun, laughter, healing, connection, guidance and transformative. Sessions with me have also been said to be a "WAKE UP call"...I often hear "You hit nail on the head."......meaning I call it out and can be blunt....the is no sugar coating and to the point always in the Intention of compassion and understanding.

Question: What evidence do you have on the survival of the human soul? Are you able to contact the soul of dead people? If so, how do you do it? What is your technique?

Answer: The only evidence of Soul survival I have is, all around...The evidence is He, She, Thee and Me. I believe everyone is a soul and all continue to live and transform co-creating the suns and moons that come to be. I do connect with the Souls of past loved One's and within each are the memories that become the affirmation within the evidence of life. We each have ancestors that came before us for we are here, co-created from love. The technique for me mainly is just being in the knowingess that we are indeed One and everyone is co-created of love....I utilize many tools through various modules embraced through my life's practices and will continue and evolve as I practice through my learning with the Universe.

I always begin in the intention to be a vessel of love in compassion and understanding.

Info Box:
www.davedbeck.com
https://twitter.com/DavedBeck
Daved@evolutionthenextlevel.com
Daved@davedbeck.com
-Best time to contact you.
Anytime via email or phone...Calls and replies are returned within 48hrs.
-Do you accept clients from foreign countries?

-Yes
-What are your fees and rates in general?
-How much do you charge?
-1 hr phone session - $160.00
30-minute phone session – $85.00
15-minute - $45.00
Periodically I post coupons and discounts.
I also offer in-person, group, corporate events and house readings/cleansings. I also offer life coaching packages co-created for a client's personal needs and goals to support their journey in the next level of evolution. Evolution is a journey of change. The Next Level is aligning head, heart, human and spirit.

*** *** ***

Vickie Gay

245

Brief bio and personal statement by Vickie Gay: I am a full time psychic medium. I am a speaker, do workshops, séance, and readings. I work with local and international clients over the phone and seen live at Expos. I have 22 years experience.

I am American and live in California. I am the USA Organizer for Parafest "Universal Passing Over 2006" a world event. This event is held simultaneously in the United States, United Kingdom, Canada, and New Zealand.

I received certificates for completing courses in mediumship and healing from the Morris Pratt Institute.

Vickie Gay: The world of spirit is all around us.

Question: What is the most important revelation or message you have received from the world of spirit? And in your opinion, where is located the world of spirit. And what the souls of dead people and other spirits do in the after life?

Answer: The most important revelation is the fact that there is no death. Life continues on. Those in the world of spirit want to talk with us, they want to help us, their personality and feelings for us does not change after the change called death. The world of spirit is all around us vibrating at a much higher rate making it invisible to the human eye. Souls of the dead, and other spirits continue to grow and evolve in the spirit world.

Question: How would/could you help your clients?
Via guidance? Spiritual comfort? Giving them messages from the world beyond? Foreseeing their future? Or?

Answer: In making a connection with the so-called dead I bring though information identifying, the spirit's name, birthday, date of passing, how they passed, how they are related to the client. The similarity pretty much ends there. Each conversation with a loved one in the spirit world is different, just as each is different with people encounters here on the physical.

Information comes though to solve problems, reassure love, forgiveness, healing, future and present events that are destiny with timelines and chain of events foreseeing into the future with guidance, answers to questions and direction.

Comfort comes knowing loved ones are still living and the fear of death is removed.

Question: What evidence do you have on the survival of the human soul? Are you able to contact the soul of dead people?
If so, how do you do it? What is your technique?

Answer: Evidence come with communicating identification, information only they know, speaking the words in phrases and lingo they used when here on the physical.

I contact the so called dead people by getting into the quiet, raising my vibration, feeling seeing hearing smelling repeat what I hear them say in the first person, and if it feels safe and comfortable I allow them to take over my body to express them self. I have been told "It is as if you become the spirit I am communicating with."

Info Box:
E-mail: mail@vickiegay.com
Telephone 415-244-6321
-Best time to contact you.
-9AM to 5PM
-Do you accept clients from foreign countries?
-Yes
-What is your website? www.vickiegay.com
-What are your fees and rates in general?
-How much do you charge?
-Expo Live Readings are $320.
For 1 hour and Phone Readings are $225.
 For 1 hour Recording of your reading $25.

*** *** ***

Jennifer Wallens

Brief bio and personal statement by Jennifer Wallens: I am a Certified Psychic and Medium with the AFCPM, full time Psychic and Medium, Animal Communicator, Spirit Artist and Paranormal Investigator. I also teach all aspects of Mediumship, Animal Communication and Psychic Development and hold classes and workshops in Las Vegas where I currently reside.

I also travel in the US and internationally doing Mediumship demonstrations, private Spirit Circles and workshops. I also work with the Route 66 Paranormal Investigators in Arizona and Nevada.

I have been a trusted and caring evidential Psychic Medium and teacher for over 20 years. She also has over 25 years experience as an environmental scientist and a biologist and is very much concerned with obtaining evidence and facts regarding proof of life after death. She was trained in the Spiritualist tradition and is grateful for this disciplined training which allowed her to learn from the very best ethical and evidential mediums in the world.

I have a Bachelors degree in Environmental Sciences and is a member of the (SNU) Spiritualists National Union, the SNUI-International (SNUI). I am featured in the ESPsychics.com and the Best Psychic Directory and listed in the top ranks of Worlds and USA Best Psychics and Mediums, as well as Number 1 Animal Communicator in 2014. I was also honored by being put on the cover of American Psychic and Medium Magazine - Jan 2014 I am so honored to be given the prestigious Lightworker Lifetime Achievement Award.

Previously I was selected as one of the top 4 Psychics in the Worldwide competition on the popular TV show *"Battle of the Psychics -War of the Worlds"*, Битва экстрасенсов on the STB Channel in 2011 in the Ukraine and was the first American to do so. I was chosen as "Best Psychic" of week 5 by the jurors during the filming of the series. Aside from 6 months of filming the TV series in the Ukraine, I have traveled extensively demonstrating my mediumship abilities in front of live audiences and on several radio programs. I will be touring the US, UK and Australia in 2015-2016.

Question: What is the most important revelation or message you have received from the world of spirit? And in your opinion, where is located the world of spirit. And what the souls of dead people and other spirits do in the afterlife?

Jennifer Wallens: The World of Spirit is truly all around us, only vibrating at a different rate.

Answer: The most important revelation I have received from the Spirit World is the acknowledgment that life is everlasting and our souls continue and are able to connect with us after death.

I believe the World of Spirit is truly all around us, only vibrating at a different rate so as to be nearly invisible. I was once shown a vision of looking beneath my feet on the earth and seeing a whole other amazingly beautiful world directly on the opposite side. I have been told Spirits do many of the same things on the other side as we do here, such as going to school, helping others on both sides and learning new things.

Question: How would/could you help your clients? Via guidance? Spiritual comfort? Giving them messages from the world beyond? Foreseeing their future? Or......?

Answer: I help my clients in many ways depending on their needs and always allow time for questions.

As a practicing Spiritual Medium, I am able to be of service to those who wish to have communication with those who have passed on, to provide evidential information from deceased loved ones. I communicate with those who have crossed over, as well as my spirit guides and those of my clients to give the messages they wish to relay through clairvoyance, clairaudience and clairsentience.

I also can draw those who may impress my mind with how they looked, and provide Spirit Portraits and Auragraphs which is a wonderful way to present a clients life reading and help them with present day difficulties.

I also can connect with dear deceased pets to help my client understand their pet is OK and the love is always there between them. I love connecting with animals here on earth as well as Interspecies Communication is most fascinating and helpful for both Human and animal.

As a Medium I am able to direct healing energies and receive information from Spirit for my clients.

On a psychic level, I can relate information regarding aura, physical condition, life situations, job, spiritual assessments, pets, relationships, family, finances, past life situations, life path and future potentials or trends.

Jennifer Wallens: I do not call in Spirits I just remain open quietly and listen to allow them to connect if they wish.

Question: What evidence do you have on the survival of the human soul? Are you able to contact the soul of dead people? If so, how do you do it? What is your technique?

Answer: I am able to connect with the souls of the deceased as well as beloved pets.

I learned my technique through the Spiritualist Churches. After doing thousands of Mediumship readings I am thoroughly convinced of the Afterlife.

My technique is to be well rested and eat healthy, then to start with a prayer and then take a few deep breaths and focus on raising my vibration to attune to the Spirit World and then open myself to communications with a clients loved ones in the Spirit World.

252

Jennifer Wallens with medium Tony Stockwell at the Arthur Findlay College farewell dance party.

I do not call in Spirits I just remain open quietly and listen to allow them to connect if they wish. It is always their free will and choice. I do require a Spirit to bring forth enough evidential information to prove who they are during a reading as well as relay any important messages specific to my client to help with the Grief and healing process.

Info Box:
Contact: info@jenniferwallens.com
702-334-6675
@MediumatLarge on Twitter
Psychic Medium Jennifer Wallens on Facebook
-Best time to contact you.
-M-Sat 9-5 pst
-Do you accept clients from foreign countries?
-Yes, Skype is wonderful for my International clients
-What is your website? Jenniferwallens.com

Jennifer Wallens with George Noory of Coast to Coast am at the International Remote Viewing Conference in 2014.

-What are your fees and rates in general?
-How much do you charge?
-My Fees vary and are always posted on my Website on my Services/Book a reading Page. They range from $150-$350. I also offer Specials during the year to reduce the cost of readings and to help my clients. I wish I didn't need to charge much or anything for my work but I am supporting myself and by doing so I am able to work full time as a Lightworker.

*** *** ***

Jessicca Haas

Brief bio and personal statement by Jessicca Haas: I was born as an Empathic Indigo Psychic Medium, and a mother to children with abilities as well. I have been in practice for 14 years now. I also love to teach others what I know about all things metaphysical. I live in the United States, but I work with and read for people of all walks of life. My specialty is reading irises, (what I do is not iridology) I am a pioneer in that modality.

Jessicca Haas: Negativity/evil is a human perception.

Question: What is the most important revelation or message you have received from the world of spirit. And in your opinion, where is located the world of spirit. And what the souls of dead people and other spirits do in the after life?

Answer: The most important revelation I have recieved from the world of spirit is that negativity/evil is a human perception, and it's a necessary ingredient to the balance of life. The point of life, why we are here, what is our purpose, is very simple. It is to gain experience, to explore every single facet of human emotion, before we are rejoined together, to the source of all energy. That source, is called many different things. My belief is that it is just a frequency, a vibration of energy that never dies or fades, just changes. Heaven is inside of us, but so is Hell, you choose what you live, you manifest your own greatness.

Question: How would/could you help your clients? Via guidance? Spiritual comfort? Giving them messages from the world beyond? Foreseeing their future? Or......?

Answer: The way I help my clients is to read their tarot cards, or make a mediumship connection with their loved ones that have passed thru the veil, to show them love lives on.

If I have a clear, close and well lit picture of their eyes, I can read their iris threads. It depends highly on the quality of the picture taken, and also on the individual iris, but some things I am able to see using that modality are: number of past lives, origin of the soul, what your abilities are, things that have impacted you greatly on the soul level. I am currently writing a book to try and teach this modality. I love to teach those willing, all I can.

Question: What evidence do you have on the survival of the human soul? Are you able to contact the soul of dead people? If so, how do you do it? What is your technique?

Answer: I believe my grandma was very psychic, I also believe I had a telepathic bond with her. Unfortunately she died when I was eleven and she didn't get a chance to teach or pass along much information to me. At that tender age, I set out on a quest to reconnect with her, as I believed our bond was stronger than death.

When I saw her waving to me as they loaded her casket into the hearse on the day of her funeral, I knew I was right. This is my first recollection of my abilities, and my first proof that love, and the soul lives on. I believe anyone can make the connection as well, if they just think of their loved one, they will gravitate to those memories. I believe it's as simple as recognizing the signs and symbols they put in your path for you to notice.

Info Box:
I can be found on www.espsychics.com for general readings, at their current rates. If you'd like to explore an Iris Reading or would like to learn from my insight I can be found on Facebook at: https://m.facebook.com/profile.php?id=1374342306171515
Iris Readings are $50.00 US currency.
I accept PayPal, my address is: jessicca8178@gmail.com

*** *** ***

Tara Mead

Brief bio and personal statement by Tara Mead: "I am a Spirit Photographer/Scrying Medium and Grief Healer. I am an American presently living in Southern California. I work locally and on occasion internationally. I conduct photography sessions as I channel spirits. I have a lifetime of experience especially within the last ten years I feel I have almost perfected the art of my spirit photography and communication with the other side on a much deeper level and taking a scientific and forensic approach to everything that I do. A long distance session will consist of my channeling the Spirit as the person taking up to 20 pictures on their end. They send them directly to me. I locate the Spirit and then send them back the photo they had taken along with whom ever I see within it. A photo was sent to me, I returned it along with two men found in her photo. I said the photo of the man on her wall was the one in the picture and the other man was located on her. The man that matched the photo on the wall was the photo sent to me and it was the man's funeral. The other man located on her passed away as well."

*** *** ***

The most important message that I have received from the Spirit world is when a loved one passes away and you feel left and alone. Spirit tells me that: You are on your own but never alone!» Spirits/Family or loved ones are always with us. We feel them, see them and at times we smell their scent. Not all of us go through these senses but know that they are there.
I believe the Spirit world is Universal, not only tied to the heavens or earth but to every being in existence. My Psychic gift of Spirit Photography and photographing the other side shows me that many beings non human, extra terrestrial's and spirits gather together.
I believe that in the afterlife we are all together as one. Through my studies and investigations also communication with the other side, the Heaven's appear to be a great deal like earth.
The difference is it's beautiful. No pain or illness, no anger only love. Family and friends gather together with Jesus the Angels and Saint's that fill us with God's everlasting love and strength made for all.

Tara Mead: The reason that I have this gift from above is to help those in need of grief healing.

Helping clients has been one of the largest accomplishments on my lifetime. Given the ability to connect with spirits that have passed away and then have the family member or client identify their loved one's or spirit in one our more of my photographs as we conduct sessions together. The client immediately runs for a photograph that matches the face of the person/spirit that we are trying to connect with.

We then compare the two pictures.A forensic view is always taken. Nose, eyes and chin or shape of their face.

This is an important process! Teeth are seen clearly and eyes as well. They are not always perfectly clear as I'm sure they do their best to appear and this takes energy. Spirits come to let is know that they are safe and with family on the other side. Most of my spirits come through with a smile on their face. Some people and me their own photographs and ask me what do I see in this. Must see the usual, I see faces. One photo was sent that was a photo of a dog. I saw a young girl.Client responds...Their daughter had passed away. Reading photos is part of what I do as well as connect and document with photograph.This process heals so very deeply!

Tara Mead: The imprint of the Spirit will never be forgotten.

Seeing is believing! Validating psychics during a reading is incredible and valuable for both myself and the psychic. As the psychic communicates with a certain spirit, I tend to get that spirit in the photo. They are not always friends or family!

At times unwanted spirits dwell in a person's home causing problems. As I detected angry and forceful faces in a photo the psychic stated we have a nasty male spirit here. Each case has a beautiful ending add the client is educated about the other side and shown that family Never Leaves! I've done this more than once with the same client showing that his wife is him.This is visual healing! Visual healing lasts beyond the death of a loved one. It helps us with the anticipation of our own passing.

On evidence of the survival of a soul:

I take a very scientific approach to any evidence collected. Photographs, EVP'S, DVR footage. Seeing, hearing or feeding a spirit is an individual's experience. A great desk of documented evidence has been collected over the years.

I believe in extra terrestrial beings because I photograph them. Spirits are with us as I photograph them as part of my collected evidence. EVP or Electronic voice phenomenon. I have numerous answers from spirits. Video recordings and DVR footage.The DVR had shown me how an orb may show signs of intelligence. I also stop the DVR and screen shot to look at faces or figures. My technique is my best form of evidence. Families identify their passed on loved ones on my photos.

I am given a picture of their family member in a photo from their life. A birthday or any photo. WWll soldier's match their families old yellowed copy of the obituary. What I do is channel a spirit, being empathic breaks my heart but helps me feel for them mute deeply in order to connect. I ask the passed on friend or loved one with respect to please be in the photos taken to help heal the broken hearted person with loneliness, anger and sorrow due to their passing. I take I'll to twenty or more photos at time. This may be around the client or their home. I'll do this day or night but it is easier during the evening hours.

I also take pictures in the mirrors. This process is called Scrying: also called seeing or crystallomancy. Seeing or Scrying is the practice of looking into our photographing in my case into translucent materials. Mirrors or water our glass are also used. This is the oldest firm of divination. This is how I conduct my practice.

Info Box:
E-mail: taravioscamead@gmail.com
tlmead2001@yahoo.com
My charges are $200.00 per hour for local clients.

*** *** ***

The Jewels of the Crown!

If I had to vote:
Obviously, I did not vote at the New York International Vote 2014-2015. I couldn't vote, because I wanted to remain impartial. And if I had to vote, the following American lightworkers would be on my list:

Angela Bixby
Anita Rosenberg
Corbie Mitleid
Daved Beck
Dena Flanagan
Diane Hiller
Gretta Alexander
Irene Hope Burke
Jennifer Shackford
Jennifer Wallens
Jessicca Cannon Haas
Jethro Smith
John Cappello
Karina Voroshilova
Kimberly Ward
Linda Carney
Linda Messerman
Lorie Johnson
Lorraine Roe
Melissa Berman
Melissa Stamps
Michelle Whitedove
Micki Dahne
Patrice Cole
Patti Negri
PennyC
Robert Rodriguez
Shannon Leischner
Sherie Hurd Roufusse
Sunhee and Chinhee Park
Suzanne Grace
Tara Viosca Mead
Tarah Harper
Tracy Lee Nash
Vickie Gay
Yolanda Billings

Statistics by the American Federation of Certified Psychics and Mediums, New York

- Approximate annual earnings of men who have consulted a psychic: $40,000/$95,000 a year
- Approximate annual earnings of women who have consulted a psychic: $20,000/$100,000 a year
- Men average age: Between 27 and 54
- Women average age: Between 21 and 60
- How much money women are willing to spend on a psychic/medium: Up to $5,000
- How much money men are willing to spend on a psychic/medium: Up to $2,000
- Percentage of men who ask their psychic to "put a spell or a curse" on somebody: 3%
- Percentage of women who ask their psychic to "put a spell or a curse" on somebody: 51%
- Percentage of men who admit to have contacted a psychic: 39%
- Percentage of women who admit to have contacted a psychic: 69%
- Percentage of men who would recommend consulting a psychic: 28%
- Percentage of women who would recommend consulting a psychic: 68%
- Percentage of divorced women who have consulted a psychic: Between 57% and 63%
- Percentage of divorced men who have consulted a psychic: Between 21% and 29%
- Percentage of women who would consult more than one psychic: 13%
- Percentage of men who would consult more than one psychic: 3%
- Percentage of women who would consult a psychic on sentimental matters (Data 2011-2012): 85%
- Percentage of men who would consult a psychic on sentimental matters (Data 2011-2012): 11%

- Percentage of women who would consult a psychic on career/professions matters (Data 2011-2012): 35%
- Percentage of men who would consult a psychic on career/professions matters or related financial projects (Data 2011-2012): 10%
- Percentage of women who would consult a psychic more than once: (Data 2011-2012): 53%
- Percentage of men who would consult a psychic more than once: (Data 2011-2012): 11%
- Approx. number of women in the United States who have spent more than $1000 for psychic reading in 2011-2012: 575,000
- Approx. number of men in the United States who have spent more than $1000 for psychic reading in 2011-2012: 95,000
- Approx. number of women in the United States who have spent more than $5000 for psychic reading in 2011-2012: 375,000
- Approx. number of men in the United States who have spent more than $5000 for psychic reading in 2011-2012: 5,000
- Approx. number of women in the United States who have spent more than $10,000 for psychic reading in 2011-2012: 275,000
- Approx. number of men in the United States who have spent more than $10,000 for psychic reading in 2011-2012: 300
- Approximate annual earning of a very successful psychic/medium in the United States: Over $5,000.000
- Number of female psychics who have consulted other psychics on personal matters: Approximately 67%
- Number of male psychics who have consulted other psychics on personal matters: Approximately 13%
- Percentage of psychics/mediums who speak any foreign language: 2%
- Percentage of female psychics/mediums who have earned an accredited college degree: 17%
- Percentage of male psychics/mediums who have earned an accredited college degree: 27%

- Approximate number of female psychics/mediums who have purchased fake degrees, including Doctor of Metaphysics, Doctor of Divinity, Doctor of anything: 111
- Approximate number of male psychics/mediums who have purchased fake degrees, including Doctor of Metaphysics, Doctor of Divinity, Doctor of anthing: 98
- Approximate number of ordained (Minister) female psychics/mediums in the United States: 217
- Approximate number of ordained (Minister) male psychics/mediums in the United States: 98
- Approximate number of psychics/mediums who would not give you their address (Home or office): 111
- Percentage of psychics/mediums who would not give you a refund: 97%
- Percentage of psychics/mediums who own a home: 83%
- Percentage of psychics/mediums who would travel long distances: 68%
- Percentage of psychics/mediums who are married: 90%
- Approximate number of psychics/mediums who had troubles with the law for the past five years: 2,137
- Approx. $ amount earned by psychics/mediums who have scammed clients in 2011-2012: $200,000.000
- Approximate percentage of psychics/mediums who only use their first name or a pseudonym: 29%
- Approx. percentage of psychics/mediums who are not affiliated with any agency or membership groups: 0.1%
- Approx. number of psychics/mediums who have their own Internet radio show: 600
- Approx. number of psychics/mediums who have their real radio-station show: 98
- Approx. number of psychics/mediums who have recommended other psychic/mediums: 512
- Approx. number of psychics/mediums who have badmouthed and/or seriously criticized other psychic/mediums: 98
- Approx. number of psychics/mediums who have hired lawyers for a libel suit, whether filed with the court or not (2007-2012): 12
- Approx. number of psychics/mediums in the United States who were certified either by one person, an owner

of a website, a group or an agency, on the spot, after a few hours, or less than 2 days: 2,876

- Number of psychics/mediums in the United States who have earned a Masters degree from an accredited college/university: 27
- Number of psychics/mediums in the United States who have earned a doctorate degree from an accredited college/university: 9
- Number of psychics/mediums in the United States who are part of the entertainment and showbiz industries: 96
- Number of psychics/mediums in the United States who are published authors: 312
- Percentage of psychics/mediums in the United States who answer you first request (Your email) via a generic response: 90%
- Percentage of psychics/mediums in the United States who would not personally/directly answer your first phone call: 91%
- Percentage of psychics/mediums in the United States who would ask a third person (A press agent, a so-called agent, a secretary, etc.) to respond to your first inquiry: 89%
- Approx. number of psychics/mediums in the United States who do pro-bono work: 36
- Approx. number of clients in the United States who have retained and/or kept on consulting a psychic/medium for more than 1 year (Data: 2000-2012): 47,000
- Approx. number of clients in the United States who have retained and/or kept on consulting a psychic/medium for more than 5 years (Data: 2000-2012): 13,000
- Approx. number of clients in the United States who have retained and/or kept on consulting a psychic/medium for more than 10 years (Data: 2000-2012): 6,550
- Approx. number of members of the clergy who has consulted a psychic/medium (Data: 2000-2012): 42
- Approx. number of members of the clergy who have jointly conducted exorcism with a psychic/medium between 1990 and 2012): 6
- Approx. number of priests who consider themselves to be either psychic or medium in the United States: 12

- Approx. number of psychics/mediums in the United States who believe in God: 99.99%
- Approx. percentage of psychics/mediums in the United States who believe in UFOs: 43%
- Approx. percentage of psychics/mediums in the United States who believe in extraterrestrials & extraterrestrial life: 87%
- Approx. percentage of psychics/mediums in the United States who believe in Jesus Christ as the "Savior": 87%
- Approx. percentage of psychics/mediums in the United States who believe in the Bible as a factual account of historical events and the word of God: 89%
- Approx. percentage of psychics/mediums in the United States who believe in reincarnation: 39%
- Approximate number of psychics in the United States: 17,500

*** *** ***

American Federation of Certified Psychics and Mediums Incorporated

In early 2012, Maximillien de Lafayette created the American Federation of Certified Psychics and Mediums Inc., which is incorporated under the Laws of the State of New York.

The Federation is a state registered corporation with the New York State Department of State/Non-Profit Corporations Division, and as defined in subparagraph (a) (5) of Section 102 of the Not-for-Profit Corporation Law and Section 404 of the Not-For-Profit Corporation Law. The Federation is organized as a New York Domestic Not-for-Profit corporation.

It is organized exclusively for the purposes of developing, recognizing, certifying, and promoting the quality work of psychics, mediums, healers, and lightworkers via orientation programs, training, forums, discussions and public awareness.

The objectives and purposes of the Federation are:

1-To promote the quality work of psychics, mediums, healers and lightworkers

2-To develop and to enhance the abilities, talents and full potentials of legitimate practitioners in the field.

3-To develop, conduct and offer training programs, orientation programs, and professional materials for the better advancement of psychics, mediums, healers, spiritual advisors, lightworkers and their profession.

4-To grant official recognition and certifications for qualified practitioners in the field.

5-The public objective of the Federation is to help practitioners in the field explore and develop their full potentials and skills, and ameliorate their talents and gifts at no cost to them, and which without the help of the corporation, their work would and could not be acknowledged, made known and appreciated by the public.

Website: amcpm.org

Get your certification at AFCPM

TESTED AND CERTIFIED BY THE AMERICAN FEDERATION OF CERTIFIED PSYCHICS AND MEDIUMS INCORPORATED

Contact the Sr. VP, Patti Negri at patti@pattinegri.com

*** *** ***

A brief note About the Author's Activities in the Paranormal and Occult Disciplines

From amazon.com profile: Maximillien de Lafayette's interest in and involvement with the paranormal and metaphysics began in 1953. Although he is a lawyer (Practicing international law and intellectual property law abroad), the author of more than 2,100 books in 26 languages (Available at amazon.com), a linguist and a historian by trade, and thus, a pragmatic thinker, Maximillien's intense fascination by the occult and supernatural phenomena took him on a legendary journey to the realms of Mounawariin (Enlightened Masters), the Rouhaniyiin (The Spirituals), and Tahiriin (The Pure Ones), known to us as the Honorable Anunnaki Ulema.

Maximillien de Lafayette's was spiritually adopted and taught by the Anunnaki-Ulema in their Ma'haad (School/Center/Temple) and on the roads of enlightenment, they chose to guide him toward Tanwir, and develop his metaphysical abilities in numerous parts of the world, starting from France and Germany to India, Burma, the Himalayas, Ethiopia, Egypt and the Middle East. He received his basic training from, and was initiated by the Honorable Master Mordachai ben Zvi, the Honorable Grand Master Li, and spiritual guides of Les Peres du Triangle, and the Ramadosh Jami'yah.

He studied and taught the occult and the supernatural-psychic Dirasaat (Studies) and Kiraat (Lectures, Teachings) of the Ulema for almost fifty years.

This integral and deeply rooted metaphysical studies, training and experiments gave birth to approximately 250 philosophical, spiritual and metaphysical books and numerous encyclopedias he wrote and made available to seekers, teachers and students around the globe; to name a few (Available at Barnes and Noble, amazon, lulu.com, and thousands of booksellers and distributors around the globe):

From his most recent published books (Bestsellers):

- 19th Edition. The Book of Ramadosh: 13 Anunnaki Ulema Techniques To Live Longer, Happier, Healthier, Wealthier".

- When Heaven Calls You: Connection with the Afterlife, Spirits, 4th Dimension, 5th Dimension, Astral Body, Parallel Dimensions and the Future.
- How to Learn the Languages of the Spirits, Ghosts, Angels, Afrit, Djinns, Demons and Entities and Converse with Them
- Encyclopedic Dictionary of Spirits' Languages and Lightworkers' Terminology and Secrets you Never Knew
- Psychics-mediums' spirits séances and witchcraft: Roster of spirits, angels & demons and how to communicate with them
- How To Become An Effective Energy Healer And Master Of The Healing Touch
- How to Become an Enlightened Psychic Detective and Remote Viewer: Ulema Psychometry Lessons, Training & Techniques to locate Missing People and Identifying Places & Objects
- How to Become an Enlightened Tarot Psychic Reader and Foresee the Future
- How to Become an Enlightened Psychic, Medium and Metaphysical Master
- America & world best psychics & healers who care most about you: names, profiles, services, contact. (Hall of Fame of the Most Caring Lightworkers)
- How to Use Your Mind Power to do the Impossible: How to Positively Change your Future
- How to Read Peoples' Vibes and Know Who They Really Are Just by Looking at Them (See their Aura, Sense their Vibes, Feel their Energy
- Calendar of Hours & Days Which Bring You Bad Luck & Good Luck: How to Positively Change your Future
- Instructions and Techniques for Commanding Spirits and Communicating with Angels and Entities
- Anunnaki Ulema Techniques and Tarot Deck To See Your Future. (The world's most powerful book on the occult and foreseeing your future on Earth and in other dimensions)
- The essential Maximillien de Lafayette: The Official Anunnaki Ulema Textbook for the Teacher and the Student.

- The Anunnaki Ulema Book of Enlightenment: Metaphysical study of the path of wisdom and esoteric knowledge.

De Lafayette has to his credits more than 250 international bestsellers certified and acknowledged by amazon.com.
He is one of the world's leading linguists and authorities on the culture, civilization and legal systems of the Arab World, Islam, and the Middle East.
After the collapse of the regime of Saddam Hussein, President George Bush and The White House most brilliant political and legal minds decided to write a New Constitution for Iraq.
The White House drafted the first copy of the proposed Constitution, and asked America's most prestigious law school (Yale University, School of Law) to review the document and translate it to Arabic, later on to be submitted to the Iraqi Council, then the governing body of Iraq.
Being a scholar, a jurist, a world-renown linguist, and an exceptionally expert in these fields, Yale University School of Law commissioned Maximillien de Lafayette to translate The White House's draft of the new Constitution of Iraq.

The Book "On The Road To Ultimate Knowledge" co-authored by Dr. Ilil Arbel retraces Maximillien's spiritual and metaphysical biography, and passages from his life with the Enlightened Masters and Ascended Anunnaki-Ulema in the East and Europe. Available at amazon.com

*** *** ***

2015 BEST PSYCHICS, MEDIUMS AND LIGHTWORKERS IN THE UNITED STATES

Maximillien de Lafayette

On the cover, left column from To to B: Vickie Gay, Jennifer Wallens, Patti Negri, Patrice Cole, Tracy Lee Nash, Kimberly Ward, Jessicca Haas. Right column from T to B: Suzanne Grace, Anita Rosenberg, Diane Hiller, Yolanda Bollings, Melissa Berman, Chinhee & Sunhee Park, John Cappello, Lower row, from L to R from third photo: Corbie Mitleid, Melissa Stamps, Jethro Smith, Shannon Leischner.

2015 BEST PSYCHICS, MEDIUMS AND LIGHTWORKERS IN THE UNITED STATES

On the cover, left column from T to B: Dena Flanagan, Robert Nobles, Sherie Hurd Roufusse, Linda Messerman, Lorie Johnson, Lorraine Roe. Top row from second photo: Daved Beck, Jennifer Shackford, Karina Voroshilova, PennyC.

Most Recent Books by Maximillien de Lafayette in the field of Metaphysics, Spirituality, Mind Power, and the Occult, available worldwide:

ENCYCLOPEDIC DICTIONARY OF DJINN, SIHR AND SPIRITISM LANGUAGES. Vocabulary, Phraseology And Dictionary Of The Languages Of Sahiriin, Djinn, Afarit, Shayatiin, Spirits, Witchcraft.

550 PAGES. The world's most authoritative book on Sihr's terminology, definitions, explanation, and the secret esoteric meaning of words, spells, commands and magical writings used in summoning spirits and conversing with multi-dimensional entities.

There is no way in the world would you be able to summon and communicate with spirits, Djinns, Afarit, demons and even Noble Souls if you are not familiar with the terminology, vocabulary and phraseology of their languages and the Sihr language.

This book will teach you all of the above, and provide you with most useful phrases needed in your conversation with summoned spirits and entities. It is easy, fun, and fast! Almost 90% of the words, expressions and sentences found in this glossary/vocabulary are commonly, frequently and jointly used by Sahiriin (Sorcerers), Rouhaniyiin (Spiritists), Mounawariin (Enlightened), and practitioners of witchcraft in the Middle East, the Near East, and North Africa, to summon and to communicate with Arwaah (Spirits), Mawtah (Dead people), Djinn, Afarit, Shayatiin (Demons or Evil Entities), and various non-physical entities which have not departed yet, crossed over, and which are still trapped in Bilaya (Doomed Zones of trapped spirits of dead people, and even our beloved pets).

It is extremely important and paramount to understand that in this context, we are exclusively referring to old spirits (Arwaah) and entities which existed and still exist in the archaic spiritist realm of the ancient world of the Middle/Near East, Pre-Islam, and Islam.

Those who are familiar with dead languages and languages of the ancient world of the Middle East, Near East and Anatolia will immediately notice that many words in the spirits and etheric multi-dimensional entities' languages are frequently found in various languages and scriptures of the ancient world, such as Akkadian, Sumerian, Assyrian, Babylonian, Ugaritic, Byblos Script of Phoenicia, Ana'kh (Anunnaki's language), Aramaic, Hebrew and Arabic. Those Arwaah and entities could be summoned only if they are contacted in their ancient languages, some of which were written down and preserved in Arabic and Sahiriin texts, and shrouded in secrecy for centuries. However, our departed relatives, parents, friends and even pets could be contacted, and/or reached without using any of the Sahiriin's languages. It is very logical, since our departed ones did not speak the archaic languages of the Arwaah of the ancient world. If your departed ones spoke English, French or Spanish for instance, you can contact them in any of these languages, as long as they did not traverse yet the "40 Day Period" after they passed away. Once they have left the zone of the 40 day period to another dimension, no one, no psychic, no medium, and no practitioner of the black or white arts can contact them. In other words, if you want to contact John Doe who spoke English, in English, go ahead without hesitation, because you are using a language he perfectly understands. You can't contact him in a language he is not familiar with. Remember there are no foreign languages schools and tapes for learning a foreign language in the afterlife. If you want to contact Mr. Ahmad X or Y, who spoke only Arabic, then you must try to reach him in Arabic. And if you want to contact an ancient spirit from Babylon or Sidon, then you must communicate with that spirit in Babylonian or Phoenician. And if you want to contact a Djinn or an Afarit, then you must contact them in one of their own languages which we have included in this book.

How to Talk to Spirits, Ghosts, Entities, Angels and Demons: Techniques & Instructions: The Most Powerful Commands and Spells.

This book is unique and extremely useful for many reasons. Mainly because it provides both the beginner and experienced practitioner with the necessary guidance, methods and techniques to communicate with various kinds and categories of entities.

In addition, it instructs the seeker on how to comply with the rules and pre-requisites necessary during a séance.

The author has placed a strong emphasis on:

• The language of the spirits, ghosts, entities and Arwaah.
• What we should do when we hear the voices of entities during a séance.
• The most powerful commands we can use during a séance.

How to order the summoned entities to grant us most needed favors and assistance in urgent matters, as well as general commands pertaining to health, the removal of difficulties in getting a job, the protection of our home from evil spirits, obtaining an immediate financial relief, and so on.

The reader should pay attention to the instructions pertaining to direct conversation with summoned entities, and especially to the protocol in communicating with spirits. This is the first book ever published in the West that deals with these topics. The contents and ideas presented in this tome are based upon the teachings and lectures of enlightened masters, who have practiced this etheric art for centuries. Therefore, you should read this book with an open mind, paying extreme attention to the instructions provided by the Ulema. Contacting spirits and entities is a very serious undertaking. They will respond to you, only if you follow the spirits' protocol, as explained in the book. Needless to say, you should be patient, and keep on practicing and practicing without despair, for it may not be easy to succeed in your first séance. But eventually, you will succeed. But without practice, patience, and perseverance, you will not be able to establish a fruitful rapport with spirits and entities.

Instructions and Techniques for Commanding Spirits and Communicating with Angels and Entities.7th Edition

This is unquestionably the world's most practical and powerful instructions-book on SIHR! This is the Alpha and Omega book of Sahiriin (Sorcerers, Magicians and Spiritists of Arab Antiquity). No doubt you will succeed in summoning some of the entities, spirits and presences, if you diligently comply with the rules, and follow the instructions of the Sahiriin and the Honorable Allamah as prescribed in this book. But you have to keep in mind, that no one, nobody on Earth can summon the spirit or the soul of a dead person, without learning the secrets of SIHR as explained in this book, which was banned by Islam and the Catholic Church since its creation.

The Allamah-Sahiriin, and some of you, who have assimilated the messages and techniques of the Allamah --which are explained in this book in utmost simplicity-- will be able to reach spirits and entities who did not yet depart from the doomed zone.

They are still alive, but they do exist in a different form. And these entities include the spirits of dead people (Human beings) who are still trapped in the doomed zone. Some of them have stayed in this macabre and disturbing zone for hundreds, perhaps thousands of years. Other entities were never dead; they were created from formulae and genetic experiments, our mind will never understand or accept. Yet, they do exist. You will be able to communicate with some of these entities, summon them, ask them favors, and even command them. But who are these entities, if they are not the souls of the departed ones, the souls of dear friends, siblings, parents, and relatives, we once had, here, on Earth? You will find out!

Language of the Arwaah (Spirits): How do we talk to entities, spirits, souls, presences, etc.? They have their own language (s), and some share the same language.

For reasons we do not understand, the language of the Arwaah contains many Hebrew, Kabalistic, Ugaritic, Phoenician, Arabic, Hittite, Turkish, Sumerian, Persian, Akkadian, Chaldean, and Assyrian words. Allamah Seif El Diin said the Arwaah words found in these ancient languages, were originally and primordially taken from the Rouhaniyaat.

This volume contain a sufficient number of Arwaah phrases, words, and commands which will help you to summon and command the Arwaah. Some entities and spirits will only respond to particular commands and very precise words and Talabaat.

283

Thus, you should use the proper words and commands that they understand.

How To Become An Effective Energy Healer And Master Of The Healing Touch.

This book will show you and teach you how to become an effective and accomplished energy healer, and provide you with lessons, practical training, and step-by-step instructions on how to use the Healing Touch, find, learn, develop esoteric Energy Healing techniques which produce astonishing supernatural and paranormal results; techniques and know-how which were shrouded in secrecy for thousands of years; they are herewith introduced to the readers and the lightworkers as part of the curriculum and training/orientation programs of the American Federation of Certified Psychics and Mediums.

3rd Edition. the United States and the World's Best Psychics, Mediums, Healers, Astrologers, Palmists, Witches and Tarot Readers 2013-2014

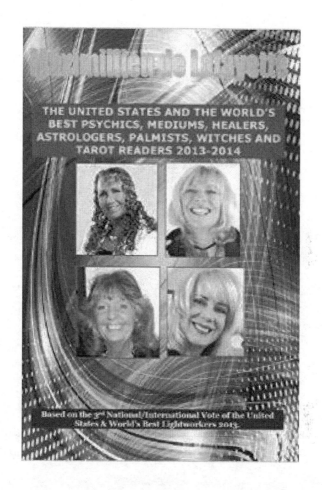

THE UNITED STATES AND THE WORLD'S BEST PSYCHICS, MEDIUMS, HEALERS, ASTROLOGERS, PALMISTS, WITCHES AND TAROT READERS 2013-2014

Based on the 3rd National/International Vote of the United States & World's Best Lightworkers 2013

3rd Edition. Published by Times Square Press in New York. "The United States and the World's Best Psychics, Mediums, Healers, Astrologers, Palmists, Witches and Tarot Readers 2013-2014" is de facto, the world's number 1 reference, source of information, and surely the most authoritative documentary book on the most popular, the most reliable, the most trusted, and best lightworkers around the globe.

The results the world rank and the national rank are based upon THE 3rd NATIONAL & INTERNATIONAL ELECTION/VOTE OF THE UNITED STATES AND THE WORLD'S BEST MEDIUMS, PSYCHICS, HEALERS, ASTROLOGERS AND LIGHTWORKERS 2013-2014.

The votes and nominations began on October 19, 2013 and ended on December 19, 2013 at midnight, New York time. It also include the winners of The Lightworkers Life Achievement Award, and the inductees into THE LIGHTWORKERS' WORLD HALL OF FAME.

REVISED EDITION. PSYCHICS, MEDIUMS AND LIGHTWORKERS YOU CAN FULLY TRUST! Their names, specialties, services, how much they charge, and how to reach them.

"Fully Trusted" means a lightworker who has demonstrated a high level of integrity, honesty and sincere commitment to clients. There are numerous distinguished practitioners who made their mark on the landscape of the occult and in esoteric fields, and reach worldwide fame, yet, in some instances, were found to be deceptive and self-serving. Unfortunately that is the "nature of the beast"!

The present book refers you to lightworkers who are sine dubio, the most honest ones who genuinely care about you. And this is what really counts. "Fully trusted" also means a lightworker who has gained the respect and trust of clients. There are numerous distinguished practitioners who made their mark on the landscape of the occult and in esoteric fields, and reach worldwide fame, yet, in some instances, were found to be deceptive and self-serving. Unfortunately that is the "nature of the beast"! The author stated "During my 50 years of involvement in spiritual matters, teaching, lecturing and authoring, I have met numerous psychics and mediums, healers and spiritual counselors, tarot readers and palmists, animal communicators and metaphysicians who were never mentioned in published works, who never appeared on television, or walked on the red carpet, yet, in my honest and professional opinion, they were/are the best, the most accomplished and the most "powerful" lightworkers of all time. Usually, enlightened teachers and practitioners are quite, and humble, and avoid pre-fabricated fame. Meticulously I have reviewed the statements of the lightworkers mentioned in this book. And I took the liberty in discussing their abilities and their success ratio with all those who sent me letters of recommendations and personal testimonies attesting to their satisfaction. I did it on purpose to satisfy my curiosity and to make sure that the clients' statements were genuine and not crafted and sent by lightworkers and/or their associates. My investigations and "fishing expeditions" brought peace to my mind. I am confident that the lightworkers who are featured in the book are honest, loving, caring and truthful to the best of their ability."

Your Lucky Hours and Unlucky Hours in Your Life From Monday To Sunday. HOW TO BRING GOOD LUCK TO YOUR LIFE.

Did you know that success and failure depend to a certain degree upon your Life's Calendar (Rizmanah) which contains the lucky and unlucky hours and days of your life? Cosmos energy and people's energy circulating during certain hours of the day have a major impact on everything you do.

287

- Each day of the week has lucky hours and unlucky hours.
- Each hour of the day corresponds to a particular or a specific activity of yours.
- If you start and/or complete any project or a business plan during the lucky hour, you will succeed at ease.
- If you do it during the opening of the unlucky hour, you will fail.
- If you are exposed to others' bad vibes during an unlucky hour, your unprotected "Zone" would be invaded, and the bad vibes would invade your zone, and hurt you. The bad vibes will bring you back luck, in the form of a failure in what you are working on.
- You have to protect your zone, feel your surrounding (Environment), and establish a barrier against others' bad vibes.
- There are general rules to establish those barriers against others' bad vibes. However, each day of the week has its own rhythm and vulnerability hours.

In this book, you will find out which, how, and why certain hours from your present and your future reveal whether you are going to be successful in your endeavors, or fail miserably. You have to read this book with an open mind, even if you are a skeptic. And just ask yourself, what if, part of this scenario could be true?

United States National Register of Tested Certified and Bona Fide Lightworkers Psychics and Mediums.

Published by Times Square Press and American Federation of Certified Psychics and Mediums, Incorporated, New York, New York. It is not an easy task to find an honest and a competent lightworker. In the United States, there are approximately 17,500 persons who claim to be a psychic, a medium, a healer, a spiritual coach, etc. The major and primordial concern of a client rotates around the credibility of a practitioner. How and where to find those exemplary, caring and competent lightworkers? The answer is here: You will find them in this book, for all of them were tested and certified by the American Federation of Certified Psychics and Mediums, Incorporated. You will never be cheated, disappointed or misled by any one of them; in other words, they are the best, the most trusted, the most credible, and above all, the friendliest.

United States National Register of Tested Certified and Bona
Fide Lightworkers Psychics and Mediums.

_____

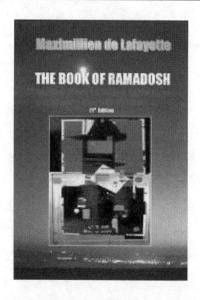

21st Edition (Condensed & Revised): THE BOOK OF
RAMADOSH. 13 Anunnaki Ulema Techniques To Live
Longer, Happier, Healthier, Wealthier.

Read this book with an open mind, for it could change your life for ever. Believing is a mystical power, however, without experimenting, you will never know the truth. The Book of Ramadosh is absolutely the most important book ever published on the supernatural powers which are dormant in all of us. The lessons and techniques of the Anunnaki Ulema are easy to understand and learn. They will open new dimensions for your mind, and help you acquire magnificent information that could lead to spectacular success in your life, relationships, business and above all, a perfect harmony with everything that surrounds you. You will never ever find these Anunnaki Ulema techniques in any other book. They are herewith presented for the first time in history by Maximillien de Lafayette. No religion, no esoteric teachings and no other spiritual master (s) have ever discussed or taught the techniques & lessons of Ramadosh.

THE "BOOK OF RAMADOSH" IS THE GREATEST BOOK ON THE POWER OF MIND, SUPERNATURAL, OCCULT, ANUNNAKI-ULEMA EXTRAORDINARY POWERS, AND HOW TO ACQUIRE AND DEVELOP EXTRAORDINARY PARANORMAL POWERS, EVER PUBLISHED IN THE WEST. Learn their techniques that will change your life for ever. You will never be the same person again. The Book of Ramadosh is based on "Transmission of Mind", used eons ago by the Anunnaki and their remnants on Earth. The book not only gives you techniques that could bring you health, happiness, and prosperity, but goes deeply into the why and how these techniques do so. Learn how to revisit past/future & travel in time/space; see dead friends & pets in afterlife; secret hour to open Conduit & zoom into your Double & multiple universes; bring luck & change your future. It includes:

Godabaari:Technique aimed at developing a faculty capable of making objects move at distance by using your mind

Gomatirach-minzari: The Minzar technique: Known as the "Mirror to Alternate Realities"
* Creating your own world

Gubada-Ari:
How to find the healthiest spots and luckiest areas on earth,

290

including private places and countries, and take advantage of this
* The Triangle of Life technique
Cadari-Rou'yaa:
The technique that develop the faculty of reading others' thoughts, intentions, and feelings. Cadari-Rou'yaa is also a method to diagnose health, and prevent health problems from occurring in the present, and in the future.
Chabariduri:
Technique/exercise to develop the faculty of remote viewing
Daemat-Afnah:
* Technique/exercise for how to stay and look 37 permanently
* Understanding human life-span and our body longevity
* The brain motor
* Vibrations, frequencies, and luck in life
* The Conduit: Health/youth/longevity
Da-Irat:
This technique eliminates stress, through one's self-energy. In other words, it is an Ulema technique used to energize one's mind and body, and to eliminate worries that are preventing a person from functioning properly everywhere, including office, school, home, hospital, social gatherings, etc.
Dudurisar:
The ability to rethink and examine past events in your life, change them, and in doing so, you create for yourself a new life and new opportunities.
To a certain degree, it is like revisiting your past, and changing unpleasant events, decisions, choices, and related matters that put you where you are today.
Arawadi:
Technique to develop a supernatural power that allows initiated ones to halt or send away difficulties, problems and mishaps into another time and another place, thus freeing themselves from worries, anxiety and fear
Baaniradu:
The healing touch technique. Touch them & heal them
Bari-du:
The technique allows you to zoom into an astral body or a Double

---

Based upon The 4th national & international election/vote of the United States and the world's best mediums, psychics, healers, astrologers and lightworkers 2014-2015. The national and international vote began on September 25, 2014 and ended on November 25, 2014 at 1:00 AM New York Time.

Before you call any psychic, medium, astrologer, lightworker, find out first if his/her name is in this book. It's your money. Be cautious. Be smart. Play it safe!! Avoid scammers! The results are not based upon packaged fame, TV, radio and media's propaganda, and maximum exposure organized and promoted by public relations firms and agents, but rather on consumers, clients, and the general public recommendations, satisfaction, and ultimately, their votes.

It includes:
* Lightworkers from 83 countries took part in this event
* Best lightworkers in the Netherlands
* Best psychics & mediums in the UK
* Best psychics & mediums in France
* Best psychics & mediums in the US
* The world's most recommended lightworkers
* The world's best metaphysical teachers
* Lightworkers of the year
* Lightworkers World Hall Of Fame: The greatest lightworkers of our times
* Best internet psychics and mediums directories and agencies
* Best mediums in the world
* Best physical mediums in the world
* Best psychics in the world
* Best tarot readers in the world
* Best healers in the world
* Best Reiki practitioners in the world
* Best pet Reiki practitioners in the world
* Best crystal & stone energy and healing practitioners
* Best astrologers in the world.
* Best numerologists in the world
* Best witches (white magick) in the world
* Best pet psychics/animal communicators in the world
* Best palmists in the world
* Best Feng Shui practitioners in the world
* Best spirit artists in the world
* Best psychic detectives in the world (crimes and missing persons)
* Best dream interpreters in the world

* World's best spirit photographers-scrying mediums
* World's best life coaches-psychics
* Best paranormal researchers/investigators in the United States
* Best ghost hunters/personalities in the United States
* Best paranormal radio show hosts in the United States
* Best paranormal TV shows in the United States
* World's best psychics' TV shows offering live reading
* Best paranormal radio shows in the world
* Best intuitive entertainers in the United States

THE SUPERSYMETRIC MIND: Activation of the Conduit and the Supersymetric Mind: Beyond the Third Eye and Toward the Oneness.

Oh yes, your guardian angel is watching over you, so keep on spreading goodness and beauty around you.
But neither goodness nor beauty alone is enough to enlighten your mind, and guide you toward the path of wisdom and ultimate knowledge.
You need to reach the zone of "Oneness", to activate your "Conduit" and dig deep into your Supersymetric Mind. Many students and friends have asked me if there is an immediate way to solve the harsh financial problems they are facing;

some sort of an Anunnaki Ulema relief-technique to bring them wealth, make them succeed in business, get rid of their troubles, and reach their goals.

The enlightened masters told us that there is only one way, one technique, one method to reach Alsoudk (Truth) and Iftirach (Happiness), which are the most important reasons, cause and effect of our intellectual and spiritual ascension. And through this ascension, our eyes will open up, our mind will develop, our heart will expand, and our being, physically, spiritually and mentally will enter the zone of ultimate knowledge; a knowledge which is an intricate part of the state of "Oneness", reachable only through our "Conduit" and "Supersymnetric Mind".

Yes, of course, enlightenment could be achieved differently, using alternative methods and paths, as explained by Brahmans, Lamas, Gurus, Swamis, Senseis, spiritual guides, and others. But no path and no alternative method are as sublime and flawless as the Anunnaki Ulema's Tarika (Road or Way of Knowledge).

And yes, you can walk on that road, and reach the hill of light, if you get rid of the Tabi'a, the lowest level of your mind, where the human nature is stained by weaknesses, nourished with vanity and greed, and solely breeds on attachment to materialistic values.

When you confer with your "Supersymetric Mind", and when you activate your "Conduit", even partially, you will be able to accomplish the quasi-impossible.

This book is not the ultimate and entire mental and esoteric arsenal you need in your fight against ignorance, nor the Alpha and Omega of the enlightenment Tarika, but it could help you a lot in finding and developing extraordinary mental and supernatural powers you had within you since you were born, but you never knew that you had them, or you could have used them when you needed an immediate relief, a helping hand, and a strong shoulder to lean on.

This book will show you a few techniques that could activate part of your "Conduit", and teach you how to converse with your "Supersymetric Mind", which is the original blueprints of your intelligence (Hidden and known), and the amazingly vast depot of knowledge and know-how, which were given to you, but you have never used, simply because you didn't know that such depot did exist, and you were rightfully entitled to have access to.

Your mind is a magnificent tool, a superb machine, an unimaginable instrument you can use to solve lots of problems on so many levels, to strengthen your faith in yourself, and to reach for the stars. Those stars are not very far away from you, for you can reach them, for you can touch them, if you use your Conduit and "Supersymetric Mind".

However, your mind would not allow you to activate the Conduit, and accomplish Anunnaki-Ulema extraordinary deeds, if you are not pure and noble in spirit and intentions.

You got to be pure goodness, forgiving, generous, sincere and humble, if you want to succeed in these esoteric studies.

Give this book a try, should we say, give yourself a try, and become a shining star in the firmament of the Oneness.

How to Use Your Mind Power to do the Impossible: Esoteric techniques to activate the mental power of your mind.

"How to Use Your Mind Power to do the Impossible" provides you with techniques that could help you discover, sense, and direct the power of your mind.

Quite often, spiritual teachers, guides, channelers, psychics, mediums and healers talk about that un-je-nesais-quoi "Energy"! But rarely, do they explain in simple terms, what that energy is! What is made from?

How energy is created? How energy could be sensed and directed?

How to use it to create a positive environment? How to use energy to block others' negative thoughts and unhealthy energy? Can we see others' energy?

Can we see our own energy?

And, can we measure energy?

If pertinent answers and explanations are not given to us, then, kiss goodbye that energy, and all the mambo-jumbo lectures of the spiritual masters and so-called psychics.

And, it's as simple as that.

In order to develop the mental power of our mind, we must first, discover the energy of our mind and body. This discovery could be achieved through Ikti-Chafa, which the author has explained at length in the book.

All of us possess what others call "supernatural powers." In fact, there is nothing "supernatural" at all. It is a matter of discovering and understanding how mental vibrations are created and transmitted. The book offers techniques which will enable you to use the power of your mind over matter.

It is not an easy task, but it could be done if you practice and persevere.

In addition to discovering and animating the power of your mind (Mental energy), you must absolutely understand how Mintaka Difaya works.

Mintaka Difaya is related to "Protecting your Zone", the physical and mental zone that surrounds your body.

Without such protection, our mental power will remain minimal. There is a wonderful technique in the book which will enable you to accomplish this task.

*** *** ***

Maximillien de Lafayette

THE WHOLE
TRUTH ABOUT
THE AFTERLIFE

A mother talking to her son from beyond the grave.
A book that will change for ever... Your life, your religious
beliefs, and everything you were taught about God, death, your
soul, and the afterlife.

SIHR DJINN AFARIT AND HOW TO SUMMON THEM.
THE BANNED BOOK OF SORCERY, SPELLS, MAGIC AND
WITCHCRAFT

WITCHCRAFT AND LIGHTWORKERS ULTIMATE TECHNIQUES TO REMOVE CURSES AND STOP THE EFFECTS OF BADMOUTHING.

The World's Ultimate Book on Sihr and Witchcraft!!
This book has multiple purposes and objectives, such as (To name a few):
• 1-Neutralizing the effects of badmouthing, the negative rumors people spread about you, and their vicious gossip: Many of our problems, headaches and suffering are caused to a certain degree by jealousy, hatred, envy, badmouthing, and –to those who believe– by what some of us call "bad luck", while others think it is a curse, which blocks our progress, prevents us from going further, and brings catastrophes to our lives.
• 2-Removing all kinds of curses. The book offers step-by-step instructions to accomplish these tasks.

300

From the contents:
• The fastest and most effective ways and esoteric techniques to remove a curse
• Everything around you affects your life and could produce a curse!
• Conditioned Curses
• Inherited Curses
• Regional Curses
• Tathiir: Cleansing and blessing a place (Home, apartment, office, etc.)
• Tools, material and accessories needed to remove curses
• How to use the language of the spirits to remove curses
• How to summon and use Afarit, Djinns, Ghools, angels and even demons to remove curses.
• Best time to set up a witchcraft séance to remove curses and find out who put a curse on you.
• Techniques which teach you how to set up your witchcraft séances.
• Instructions on how to translate a word or a sentence from any language to the languages of the spirits, angels and Afrit.
• The most effective spells and magic's commands.
• How to use Numerical Value of the names of your enemies to remove curses.
• How to build magical squares and write talismans.
• Learn witchcraft terms and concepts.
• Recommended lightworkers, psychics, mediums, healers, intuitive astrologers, tarot readers, metaphysicians, witches.
The best of the best in business. How to reach them and benefit from their services.

*** *** ***

NOTES

NOTES

NOTES

NOTES

Published by
Times Square Press
New York
www.timessquarepress.com

Printed in the
United States of America
December 13, 2014

Made in the USA
San Bernardino, CA
28 November 2015